D1233017

Kenyon College
Gambier, Ohio

Written by Jay Helmer and Zack Rosen

Edited by Adam Burns, Meghan Dowdell, and Kimberly Moore

Layout by Meryl Sustarsic

Additional contributions by Omid Gohari, Christina Koshzow, Chris Mason, Joey Rahimi, and Luke Skurman

ISBN # 1-4274-0083-0
ISSN # 1551-1036
© Copyright 2006 College Prowler
All Rights Reserved
Printed in the U.S.A.
www.collegeprowler.com

Last Updated 5/15/06

Special Thanks To: Babs Carryer, Andy Hannah, LaunchCyte, Tim O'Brien, Bob Sehlinger, Thomas Emerson, Andrew Skurman, Barbara Skurman, Bert Mann, Dave Lehman, Daniel Fayock, Chris Babyak, The Donald H. Jones Center for Entrepreneurship, Terry Slease, Jerry McGinnis, Bill Ecenberger, Idie McGinty, Kyle Russell, Jacque Zaremba, Larry Winderbaum, Roland Allen, Jon Reider, Team Evankovich, Lauren Varacalli, Abu Noaman, Mark Exler, Daniel Steinmeyer, Jared Cohon, Gabriela Oates, David Koegler, and Glen Meakem.

Bounce-Back Team: Bryan Stokes II, John Lesjack, and Emily Peters.

College Prowler®
5001 Baum Blvd.
Suite 750
Pittsburgh, PA 15213

Phone: 1-800-290-2682
Fax: 1-800-772-4972
E-Mail: info@collegeprowler.com
Web Site: www.collegeprowler.com

How this all started...

When I was trying to find the perfect college, I used every resource that was available to me. I went online to visit school websites; I talked with my high school guidance counselor; I read book after book; I hired a private counselor. Sure, this was all very helpful, but nothing really told me what life was like at the schools I cared about. These sources weren't giving me enough information to be totally confident in my decision.

In all my research, there were only two ways to get the information I wanted.

The first was to physically visit the campuses and see if things were really how the brochures described them, but this was quite expensive and not always feasible. The second involved a missing ingredient: the students. Actually talking to a few students at those schools gave me a taste of the information that I needed so badly. The problem was that I wanted more but didn't have access to enough people.

In the end, I weighed my options and decided on a school that felt right and had a great academic reputation, but truth be told, the choice was still very much a crapshoot. I had done as much research as any other student, but was I 100 percent positive that I had picked the school of my dreams?

Absolutely not.

My dream in creating *College Prowler* was to build a resource that people can use with confidence. My own college search experience taught me the importance of gaining true insider insight; that's why the majority of this guide is composed of quotes from actual students. After all, shouldn't you hear about a school from the people who know it best?

I hope you enjoy reading this book as much as I've enjoyed putting it together. Tell me what you think when you get a chance. I'd love to hear your college selection stories.

Luke Skurman
CEO and Co-Founder
lukeskurman@collegeprowler.com

Welcome to College Prowler®

During the writing of College Prowler's guidebooks, we felt it was critical that our content was unbiased and unaffiliated with any college or university. We think it's important that our readers get honest information and a realistic impression of the student opinions on any campus—that's why if any aspect of a particular school is terrible, we (unlike a campus brochure) intend to publish it. While we do keep an eye out for the occasional extremist—the cheerleader or the cynic—we take pride in letting the students tell it like it is. We strive to create a book that's as representative as possible of each particular campus. Our books cover both the good and the bad, and whether the survey responses point to recurring trends or a variation in opinion, these sentiments are directly and proportionally expressed through our guides.

College Prowler guidebooks are in the hands of students throughout the entire process of their creation. Because you can't make student-written guides without the students, we have students at each campus who help write, randomly survey their peers, edit, layout, and perform accuracy checks on every book that we publish. From the very beginning, student writers gather the most up-to-date stats, facts, and inside information on their colleges. They fill each section with student quotes and summarize the findings in editorial reviews. In addition, each school receives a collection of letter grades (A through F) that reflect student opinion and help to represent contentment, prominence, or satisfaction for each of our 20 specific categories. Just as in grade school, the higher the mark the more content, more prominent, or more satisfied the students are with the particular category.

Once a book is written, additional students serve as editors and check for accuracy even more extensively. Our bounce-back team—a group of randomly selected students who have no involvement with the project—are asked to read over the material in order to help ensure that the book accurately expresses every aspect of the university and its students. This same process is applied to the 200-plus schools College Prowler currently covers. Each book is the result of endless student contributions, hundreds of pages of research and writing, and countless hours of hard work. All of this has led to the creation of a student information network that stretches across the nation to every school that we cover. It's no easy accomplishment, but it's the reason that our guides are such a great resource.

When reading our books and looking at our grades, keep in mind that every college is different and that the students who make up each school are not uniform—as a result, it is important to assess schools on a case-by-case basis. Because it's impossible to summarize an entire school with a single number or description, each book provides a dialogue, not a decision, that's made up of 20 different topics and hundreds of student quotes. In the end, we hope that this guide will serve as a valuable tool in your college selection process. Enjoy!

OMID GOHARI ○ CHRISTINA KOSHZOW ○ CHRIS MASON ○ JOEY RAHIMI ○ LUKE SKURMAN ○
The College Prowler Team

KENYON COLLEGE
Table of Contents

Introduction from the Authors

When I go home to New York, people ask me where I go to college, and when I reply, "Kenyon," I inevitably get one of two responses. The first is a puzzled expression, to which I have to add "it's a small school in middle-of-nowhere Ohio." The latter group, which is the majority, know Kenyon for what it is—one of the premier small liberal arts schools in the country. If recent years are any indication, the group that hasn't heard of Kenyon is rapidly shrinking.

They know it for English and swimming, which is the school's traditional bread and butter, and while those areas remain strong, Kenyon is diversifying its strengths. Several years ago, the school built a state-of-the-art $30 million science quad that has increased the proportion of science majors at Kenyon. Recently, the school broke ground on a $60 million athletic facility that will be among the best in Division III, and rival some Division I schools. The word is out. In just five years, the admissions rate has gone from two-thirds to below 50 percent, and Kenyon is gaining the national recognition usually reserved for East Coast schools with billion dollar endowments.

With all of these changes, one might think that Kenyon is a drastically different place than when Kenyon's founder and first president Bishop Philander Chase first climbed Gambier Hill in 1829. However, nothing could be further from the truth. When walking down Middle Path into "downtown" Gambier, one still feels as though it is a college nestled in nature fit for a Robert Frost poem. Over 170 years later, the school has made some additions, namely women (including our first female president), telephones, and the Internet; however, the traditional feel remains the same. That's what Kenyon students love about their school. Other schools claim they are unique; Kenyon actually is.

I am here because my guidance counselor told me to go listen to a Kenyon recruiter. It was only when I made the trip to the place that maps forgot, and walked down Middle Path, that Kenyon's beauty had me hooked. I can't imagine life anywhere else. Kenyon is a school of learning and friendship. If this sounds like your cup of tea, hopefully this book can give you a few insights to life on the hill.

Jay Helmer and Zack Rosen
Authors, Kenyon College

By the Numbers

General Information
Kenyon College
Ransom Hall
Gambier, Ohio 43022

Control:
Private

Academic Calendar:
Semester

Religious Affiliation:
Episcopal

Founded:
1824

Web Site:
www.kenyon.edu

Main Phone:
(740) 427-5000

Admissions Phone:
(800) 848-2468

Student Body
**Full-Time
Undergraduates:**
1,611

**Part-Time
Undergraduates:**
23

**Total Male
Undergraduates:**
767

**Total Female
Undergraduates:**
867

Admissions

Overall Acceptance Rate:
38%

Early Decision Acceptance Rate:
72%

Regular Acceptance Rate:
36%

Total Applicants:
3,808

Total Acceptances:
1,462

Freshman Enrollment:
467

Yield (% of admitted students who actually enroll):
32%

Early Decision Available?
Yes

Early Action Available?
No

Regular Decision Deadline:
January 15

Regular Decision Notification:
April 1

Early Decision Deadline:
December 1

Early Decision Notification:
December 15

Must-Reply-By Date:
May 1

Applicants Placed on Waiting List:
586

Applicants Accepted from Waiting List:
284

Students Enrolled from Waiting List:
8

Transfer Applications Received:
124

Transfer Applications Accepted:
21

Transfer Students Enrolled:
15

Transfer Application Acceptance Rate:
16%

Common Application Accepted?
Yes

Supplemental Forms?
Yes

Admissions E-Mail:
admissions@kenyon.edu

Admissions Web Site:
www.kenyon.edu/x602.xml

→

SAT I or ACT Required?
Yes, either

**SAT I Range
(25th–75th Percentile):**
1230–1420

**SAT I Verbal Range
(25th–75th Percentile):**
620–730

**SAT I Math Range
(25th–75th Percentile):**
610–690

SAT II Requirements
None required, although scores
will be considered if submitted.

Freshman Retention Rate:
93%

**Top 10% of
High School Class:**
50%

Application Fee:
$45

Financial Information

Full-Time Tuition:
$33,930

Room and Board:
$5,570

Books and Supplies:
$1,150

**Average Need-Based
Financial Aid Package:**
$23,245

**Students Who
Applied for Financial Aid:**
52%

Students Who Received Aid:
42%

Financial Aid Forms Deadline:
February 15

Financial Aid Phone:
(740) 427-5430

Financial Aid E-Mail:
daugherty@kenyon.edu

Financial Aid Web Site:
www.kenyon.edu/x8769.xml

Academics

The Lowdown On...
Academics

Degrees Awarded:
Bachelor of Arts

Most Popular Majors:
20% English
11% Social Sciences
10% History
10% Psychology
 7% Multi/Interdisciplinary
    Studies

Full-Time Faculty:
147

**Faculty with
Terminal Degree:**
97%

**Student-to-
Faculty Ratio:**
10:1

Average Course Load:
Five classes

Graduation Rates:
Four-Year: 79%
Five-Year: 83%
Six-Year: 84%

AP Test Score Requirements

Possible credit for scores of 3, 4, or 5

IB Test Score Requirements

Possible credit for scores of 6 or 7

Sample Academic Clubs

Debate Team, Math Club, Model UN

Best Places to Study

Gund study lounge, Library, Nu Phi Kappa in Ascension

Students Speak Out On...
Academics

{ **"Kenyon has a lot to offer. Because it is a small school and the student-to-faculty ratio is low, I think that in a lot of cases, the faculty and administration are willing to bend over backwards for all of the students. It is a really hard school academically."**

Q "I cannot say enough good things about the faculty at Kenyon. They are among the brightest in their fields, and they are dedicated to teaching in a way that professors at research universities simply are not. **Academically, the faculty encourages students to be skeptical** and engaged learners, but their influence goes beyond the classroom. My faculty advisor took me out to lunch to convince me to study abroad; other faculty members have taken the time to help me find summer research positions and discuss the options I have after graduation. They are excellent scholars and totally dedicated to their students."

Q "I've enjoyed the majority of the classes I've taken here. The professors are knowledgeable and interested in the subject. They want you to succeed, and are generous with their time and energy in helping you reach academic goals. For the most part, I've gotten the classes I want. Registration is very easy and non-competitive. Professors are often willing to **sign for you to enter the class, even if it's filled**."

Q "It depends entirely on the student. If you do all the homework and attempt to get something out of all the material, you will have an academic experience and feel that you are working twice as hard as everyone else. The **academics are as difficult as you permit them to be**, but as far as I understand, you actually have to work for an A, regardless of how intelligent you are. Not so for a B."

Q "Overall, the academics here are slightly below fantastic—slightly. The faculty rank as high as the academics. The **profs are great, but not the pre-eminent scholars** in their field (for the most part). The ability to get classes that you want is almost 100 percent, with the exception of English classes that fill up during major pre-enrollment."

Q "The academics are wonderful! No matter how difficult or easy your courses were in high school, Kenyon classes will challenge you to explore your horizons and think in new ways. The faculty is absolutely amazing here at Kenyon. They are outstanding scholars, and **they also invest time and emotional commitment** in their students. They really value you, the student, learning and understanding and enjoying, all at the same time. If you plan it right, you can get the classes you want. For really popular courses, there are usually several different sections, and you should list alternate times, but I don't know anyone who didn't get a class. The teachers are also really nice about this. If you come to them and say 'I really want to take this course,' they will usually let you add it."

Q "Overall, the academics are fantastic. Kenyon students often forget that, compared to 95 percent of colleges and universities, we have great teachers, challenging courses in a wide variety of subjects, and outstanding facilities. The faculty, though, differ from department to department, and are dedicated, available, and engaging. **They are great people and a great resource**. Sometimes, it can be difficult to get the classes you want, particularly in the larger departments or as a younger student, but it's not a serious problem."

Q "It is fairly easy to get into introductory classes, but I wish that it was a little bit less selective and less hard to get into creative writing classes at Kenyon. **And the English department is really well known**. I think that English majors really have to work hard to get into courses they are interested in because there is a lot of demand."

Q "I don't think the academics at any institution could be that much better than what Kenyon has to offer. From the course selection to the teachers to the intimacy in the classroom, Kenyon's classes are extremely productive and very personal. The students and teachers are familiar with one another because there are at most 15 students in most of my classes. I have incredible teachers in all of my classes, and if I don't think that I understand a certain concept, the **teachers are always available for further discussion**. Fortunately, I was able to get every class I wanted for my freshman year. Due to the size of the classes, certain classes are going to be more difficult to gain a spot, but I've been lucky to this point."

The College Prowler Take On...
Academics

It is easy to lose sight of the fact that Kenyon is a great academic school. The people are so nice and the campus is so scenic that people often forget just how hard everyone is working. A former president said that the Kenyon atmosphere is like "learning in the company of friends." There seems to be little competition, even within majors and departments, but everyone spends a lot of time learning.

The traditional selling point of Kenyon College has been its English and Humanities program. Such esteemed writers as Robert Lowell and EL Doctorow were given their educations here, and Gambier is home to *The Kenyon Review*, one of the nations premier literary journals. English is by far the most populated major, and the scope of classes offered is far-reaching. However, we are expanding from our English focus. The science quad and other changes have helped to rope in a wide range of majors. The humanities offer many classes. Kenyon's political science intro—The Quest for Justice—attracts many freshmen to the major, and the Integrated Program of Humane Studies (IPHS) gives first an overview of Western literature and philosophy and then narrows down to more specific movements, such as post-modernism or romanticism. History and classics also attract many students, and the anthropology and sociology majors are also very popular. Kenyon prides itself on its small classes and close student-professor relationships. Faculty at Kenyon place their emphasis on teaching, as opposed to research. Every professor is required to hold at least five office hours a week. Kenyon does get many big name, high-profile professors on campus, but they are not treated any differently. They too have small classes and make themselves available, even if they did write *Eddie and the Cruisers*.

The College Prowler® Grade on

Academics: A-

A high Academics grade generally indicates that professors are knowledgeable, accessible, and genuinely interested in their students' welfare. Other determining factors include class size, how well professors communicate, and whether or not classes are engaging.

Local Atmosphere

The Lowdown On...
Local Atmosphere

Region:
Midwest

City, State:
Gambier, Ohio (Knox County)

Setting:
Rural

Distance from Columbus:
1 hour

Distance from Cleveland:
2 hours

Closest Shopping Malls or Plazas:

Easton Town Center

160 Easton Town Center,
Columbus, OH

(614) 416-7000

Closest Movie Theaters:

Premiere Theaters

11535 Upper Gilchrist Rd.,
Mount Vernon

(740) 392-2220

Major Sports Teams:

Columbus Blue Jackets
(hockey)

Columbus Crew (soccer)

City Web Sites

www.mountvernonohio.org

www.villageofgambier.org

Did You Know?

5 Fun Facts about Knox County:

- At nine stories, Kenyon's own Caples dormitory is the **tallest building in the county**.
- The **New Testament Stone Garden** in Mount Vernon illustrates 14 bible passages through stones of various sizes, shapes, and weights.
- **1,110 privately owned, non-farm establishments** employ 17,032 people in Knox County.
- The Village of Centerburg, Ohio claims to be the **exact geographical center** of the state.
- Gambier is known for having **gorgeous architecture**—some of buildings date back to the 19th century.

Local Slang:

Copious – A large amount of something (copious amounts of corn grow in Gambier).

Sack – A bag.

Sketchy – A person of ill repute.

Students Speak Out On...
Local Atmosphere

"Gambier is very cute and very pretty; Mt. Vernon is very commercialized. Kenyon's location is a positive and a negative—the quaint stuff is fun for a while, but in the end, you do crave better food and more culture."

Q "Kenyon's location is definitely a plus because it is gorgeous. It's the perfect location for any student who wants to concentrate on his or her studies and have enough distractions to remain busy, but not too many to distort students' priorities. The one thing all students must be aware of is that because of Kenyon's size, or lack thereof, it's a very intense campus. **You will become familiar with almost everyone in your class**, and you will be living with them for four years. It helps a lot if you enjoy being around people!"

Q "**The village of Gambier is a charming addition** to Kenyon's sense of community, as it reminds us that we are still members of society, despite the 'Kenyon Bubble.' Everyday interactions with the post office man, bookstore workers, and bank members allow interactions that are not purely academic and force relationships that extend beyond college-age people. Mt. Vernon is adequate, although not terribly exciting, and I'd love to see more restaurants. At the same time, being so far from a major city allows us to participate in our own community in a bigger way. Location is positive, if you can handle the isolation. It gives a better focus to studies without distraction."

Q "Basically, Kenyon is the ideal college for anyone who enjoys the intimacy of a small town and **isolation from the rest of the world**. You can't always be isolated from the world, though, and Mt. Vernon, only a five-minute drive from Gambier, allows Kenyon students to re-enter the lives they may have left. If you have the patience, you learn that Mt. Vernon has anything and everything you could want or need as a college student."

Q "Once you get beyond the initial 'middle of nowhere' factor, you really begin to love the village of Gambier. Cars stop for you, everything is really clean, and you are able to interact with other students, faculty, and residents every day just walking through. Mt. Vernon, for what it is, a place to get all life's necessities, is fine. I actually like Gambier better, but Mt. Vernon is a fun random trip if you feel like it. Kenyon's location is definitely a positive. **Being surrounded by nature without a lot of distractions** lets you get your work done, and you're more likely to interact with other students more because you're not going into a city often. Plus, Columbus isn't that far away at all, and there's a big shopping mecca only 50 minutes away as well. Plus, it's just beautiful here."

Q "I came out to Kenyon to visit, and I pretty much knew what Kenyon was going to be like, and I think that you don't come to Kenyon looking for a city. You don't come to Kenyon looking for a Gap or J.Crew on the corner. That is what part of the beauty of Kenyon is. The fact that it is a **beautiful rural landscape, and it has a lot to offer** with its small community—as far as community service and reporting for the newspaper goes. There are a lot of ways students can really work with their surroundings, whereas in the big city, they might feel that they are unable to make a difference."

Q "The **village of Gambier is perhaps the world's greatest college town**—it's only a touch too small. As far as Mt. Vernon, if it weren't for Wal-Mart and Kroger, our hickish sense of civilization would be totally useless. Kenyon's location is an extreme positive. Simply put: Kenyon would not function at all outside of Gambier."

Q "The village of Gambier is incredibly small and quaint. There really isn't too much to it. Mt. Vernon is kind of hickish with a lot of Mennonites and 'middle-America' restaurants and stores. Kenyon's location is very isolated, but that's what I like about it. **It's a break from reality. Plus, Columbus is only 50 minutes away**."

Q "Gambier is very picturesque and quiet. Mt. Vernon is a good place to get away. Mt. Vernon has all the staples like McDonald's and a Wal-Mart, movie theaters, and bowling alleys, plus a pretty, historical section of town. I think Kenyon's location is a positive. If you're from a big city, it takes a little adjusting (my best friend said that there are more people in two blocks in Chicago than in the entire town of Gambier including students), but there's always Columbus if you love crowds and traffic. **The quietness of Gambier is conducive to studying**—there aren't a whole lot of procrastinating excuses in the town itself."

Q "Gambier and Knox County are what make Kenyon what it is, plain and simple, and for better and for worse. **Don't come here if you're looking for great nightlife opportunities**, world-class theaters or art, or hustle and bustle. That said, there are incredible opportunities here that you won't get in a larger campus setting—the chance to spend a lot of time with a small group of people in a beautiful rural environment."

Q "Growing up in Long Island, I was able to enjoy the mixture of both the city and country lifestyle. The village of Gambier is **definitely not a metropolis**, and that's what makes Kenyon so incredible. The students and faculty at Kenyon make up a large percentage of the residents in Gambier."

The College Prowler Take On...
Local Atmosphere

When other people complain about how small their college town is, Kenyon students just roll their eyes. While Kenyon students are modern, everything around them is in a time warp. Downtown Gambier is a single block long, and features a market, deli, bookstore, coffee shop, post office, bar, and a barber. The Amish sell crafts and produce in the fall, and sometimes a guy sells jewelry and sweaters outside of Farr Hall. Regardless, Kenyon students love it. Gambier functions as a blank canvas for Kenyon students. It is simple, slow and quiet, and any student activity stands out all the more against this backdrop. You get so used to it that even a visit to Mt. Vernon can seem jarring. If all this becomes too much to bear, there is a fair amount to do in the surrounding towns and counties. If you like things that are quaint and pretty, then you will be set. Apple picking, haunted houses, blue grass festivals, and homemade pie can all be found within a 30-minute drive of Kenyon. An hour away, Columbus offers culture, restaurants, and a variety of other diversions. Ten minutes outside the city is the Easton shopping center, which has a Cheesecake Factory, Gap, and even street signs. Any feelings of missing modern culture and convenience will be wiped away by the shiny suburban monstrosity.

All in all, the thing to stress most is that you know what you are getting in to. Students who transfer after their freshman year are the ones who thought they could force themselves to like what Kenyon is. The happiest students are the ones that knew they were going to a small school in the cornfields and looked forward to it anyway.

The College Prowler® Grade on

Local Atmosphere: C+

A high Local Atmosphere grade indicates that the area surrounding campus is safe and scenic. Other factors include nearby attractions, proximity to other schools, and the town's attitude toward students.

Safety & Security

The Lowdown On...
Safety & Security

Number of Security Officers:
10 full time, 5 part time

Kenyon Security Phone:
(740) 427-5000, or 5555 for on-campus emergencies

Safety Services:
Transportation, escort service, property engraving, campus watch, safety whistles

Health Services:
Sparrow House
221 North Ackland
(740) 427-5525
Offers basic medical and counseling services

Health Center Office Hours:
Monday–Friday
9 a.m.–12:30 p.m., and
1:30 p.m.–4:30 p.m.
by appointment

Students Speak Out On...
Safety & Security

"Safety and security seem to be sort of malicious. They don't act like they're here for our safety. They act like they're bitter and want to get people in trouble because they can."

Q "I started out as a freshman feeling as if security was always out to get me. Whether or not I was throwing a party in my room or going to a party, I always felt as if they were the enemy. As I have gone on and now am a senior, I appreciate their role; I realize they are not out to get us. They have done a lot for the school, and at least **90 percent of the time, they care about the good of the students**."

Q "**Safety and security's role is to hassle students** and to occasionally provide a helpful service. They are a presence."

Q "Safety and security crack down a lot on parties, but I don't think they're too strict. **You can always call them for a ride home**, and people take advantage of that, which is good. (They don't always do that at other schools.)"

Q "In practice, it is a truly nice convenience to be able to visit any dorm, especially at odd hours, without having to be buzzed in. Being such a small community, the **unlocked doors rarely elicit unwelcome visitors** aside from the occasional wandering drunk. The doors to individual rooms can obviously be locked for privacy and safety."

Q "I'm not too familiar with the safety and security department, but I do know **they've always been there whenever our fire alarm has gone off** (around 15 times in two months), and they are always efficient with towing cars when you leave your car alone for too long. Fortunately, I'm not too familiar with the safety and security personnel, but I did go on the campus lighting walk, which I think is an incredible idea. An electrician, a couple security officers, and students walked around the campus finding areas that were too dark. So far, I'm satisfied, and from what I've heard from the lighting walk, there are plenty of safety projects that will make the students feel even more comfortable, which is never a concern anyway."

Q "**The campus at large is very safe**, and although lighting is a concern, most girls, I believe, feel comfortable walking alone at night."

The College Prowler Take On...
Safety & Security

Kenyon is about as non-threatening as a school can get. Dorms and academic buildings stay unlocked, and people leave their backpacks unattended for hours at the library. Kenyon is an incredibly safe and trusting environment. The thefts that do happen are almost impossible to trace because they are a product of trust. People steal unlocked bikes, food in community refrigerators, and shoes from unlocked lockers.

Security is there mostly as party monitors. They check to make sure underage students aren't drinking, and that everything is up to fire code. During the day, they can be seen riding around campus in their SUVs, but there is not much for them to do. Party nights, they go through dorms and check on loud rooms, but a little common sense (no blasting music and no one screaming "I'm so drunk!") will ensure that you stay out of trouble in this respect. Security truly does care about the students. Being a 2,000-person village, Gambier doesn't really have any dark alleys or bad neighborhoods. Some of campus is poorly lit, but blue-security phones are visible in all the less populated areas. Most of the people that hang out around Kenyon are Kenyon students.

The College Prowler® Grade on
Safety & Security: A

A high grade in Safety & Security means that students generally feel safe, campus police are visible, blue-light phones and escort services are readily available, and safety precautions are not overly necessary.

Computers

The Lowdown On...
Computers

High-Speed Network?
Yes

Wireless Network?
Yes, in dorms, and Olin and Chalmers Libraries

Number of Labs:
12 including some dorms

Number of Computers:
500

Operating Systems:
Mac OS X
Windows XP

Discounted Software

None

Free Software

None

24-Hour Labs

Ascension basement lab, Gund Study Lounge, Roth Lab in the basement of Pierce

Charge to Print?

No

Students Speak Out On...
Computers

{ **"The campus computers are fine, although I barely ever use them. One should definitely bring his or her own computer. If everybody relied on the campus labs, all hell would break loose."**

Q "The college is gradually **moving towards replacing the poor computers that still exist** in the basement of Ascension and other random areas around campus. The sciences are mostly covered, while the humanities are somewhat lacking. Throughout campus, there are almost enough computers, although the library should definitely have more. I would advise bringing a personal computer, if only for personal convenience."

Q "The campus' computers are top-of-the-line. There are more than enough computers on campus to satisfy the student body, because enough students bring their own computers. I brought my computer, and it's really been helpful, but in case my laptop crashed, I would never have a problem finding another computer to use, even if it's a fellow dormmate's. I think **it would be beneficial for any student to have a computer** because it would make your life a lot easier since it's so convenient to setup a computer in your dorm and just work from home instead of walking a couple minutes away. I don't know, you can definitely survive without a computer, but if you're attached to the Internet, go ahead and bring one."

Q "While there are computers available all over campus, it's best to bring one for personal use as things can get crowded, especially around finals. **The connections are fast**, wireless is coming into certain campus buildings, and the support is available and thorough."

Q "There are a ton of computers. I think it is nice to have a computer. I don't think it is absolutely necessary. If you are going to bring a computer, it is nice to have a laptop because it gives you the flexibility of going to the library with it—it also gives you the flexibility of finding an empty classroom or study room where you can use it. I don't think it is absolutely necessary, but I think that it may be in the future. I think that **Kenyon has done a pretty good job of trying to supply 24-hour computer access** to students, and I have had very little trouble finding a free computer at pretty much every hour during the day."

Q "The computing system at Kenyon has strengths and pitfalls. On the plus side, there is Internet access for every student in his/her room, and 100-MB on the school server for each student to store files. The downside is reliability. The student drives on the server are often difficult to access from computer labs, and the e-mail server is faulty a couple of times a week."

Q "With the exception of exam time, **Kenyon has ample computer lab space**. While the computers on the main floor of the library may be difficult to snag in evening hours, the computer labs in the basement of buildings are generally available. Exam time, however, is a different animal."

Q "For the majority of the year, **it is possible to survive without one**, however, most students prefer to have the regular access to e-mail and IM that a PC allows."

The College Prowler Take On...
Computers

Like most colleges, the majority of Kenyon students own their own computers. The school provides Ethernet hookups in every room, and a blue cord that connects you both to the net and to the Kenyon network. E-mail is used often here, both for personal correspondence and college business, so being able to check your mail at your leisure is very nice. A student's room may prove to be the last place they would be able to work in peace. That is why a lot of students, even the aforementioned computer owners, do their work at many of the computer labs scattered around campus. In general, there are enough computers, and students stagger their study hours so that you will be able to find one if you need one. The more popular locations, like the library and Gund Commons, fill up quickly, but there are many "secret" computer labs scattered around campus. The basement of Ascension Hall has two such labs, as does Pierce Hall.

The only time the computer situation gets a little hairy is during finals. At this time, students come out of the woodwork to write their papers, and the competition for computers gets fierce. It is during these times that you will either stick to your own computer or be very crafty about getting an open one in the lab. Gund Commons will be a lost cause—it is not uncommon to see someone camped out there for days at a time, sometime with a pillow and blanket for naps. The library is also very difficult. Your best bet at these times is Pierce or Sam Mather.

The College Prowler® Grade on

Computers: B-

A high grade in Computers designates that computer labs are available, the computer network is easily accessible, and the campus' computing technology is up-to-date.

Facilities

The Lowdown On...
Facilities

Student Center:
The middle of town is Kenyon's true "student center," but the closest thing on campus is Gund Commons.

Athletic Center:
Kenyon Athletic Center

Libraries:
The connected Olin and Chalmers Libraries make up "the library" on campus.

Campus Size:
1,200 acres

Popular Places to Chill:
The patio in front of Farr Hall and the bookstore

What Is There to Do on Campus?

During the week, you can work in the library, go jogging down the Kokosing Gap Trail, or swim laps at Kenyon Athletic Center. At night, there is a plethora of Kenyon-sponsored "dry events" to compliment the drinking and Greek scene.

Movie Theater on Campus?

No

Bowling on Campus?

No

Bar on Campus?

Gambier Grill (behind the bookstore)

Coffeehouse on Campus?

Middle Ground

Favorite Things to Do

A lot of Kenyon's favorite activities involve simply hanging out with friends. Whether you park your scooters in the Gund patio or sit in the benches outside Farr, the school very often resembles an admissions booklet. Students sit and read magazines in the bookstore, study as groups in the library atrium, and hold hands on the bench at Sunset Point. When it snows, people sled down hills on lunch trays. There is always some event to go see, whether it is a student-produced, senior-thesis play, improv and sketch comedy, or a speaker. The campus's three a cappella groups are immensely popular, the concerts are always packed, and students will go out of their way to see them do teaser sets at various coffeehouses and fundraisers. The Kenyon Film Society (KFS) designates a theme every week (musicals, black and white, Sean Penn) and shows three movies a week on Wednesday, Friday, and Saturday. Sporting events can usually reel in some spectators, depending on the sport and the weather, and any event offering free food pretty much guarantees attendance.

Students Speak Out On...
Facilities

> "With the exception of the science quad, the school buildings are, for the most part, beautiful from the outside, and in need of a major overhaul on the inside, especially the historic South dorms, and especially of those three, Leonard."

Q "**The architecture is amazing**, but the insides of the buildings aren't all that great. I am a little bit afraid of the athetic center. I am afraid that it might take away from the role that the town now plays as a sort of student union, as a meeting place for the students. I think that is a real problem."

Q "**We don't necessarily need a student union** because I think that the library, Pierce, Town, and Gund Commons in any season is a fine and a good meeting point. It also adds to the uniqueness of the campus."

Q "**The bookstore is amazing**. The buildings are beautiful. I love Ascension. The state-of-the-art fitness facility is by far the nicest building we have on campus. I know people who go there two or three times a day."

Q "The village is a part of the college, and only time will tell how much the village will play a part in my Kenyon experience. **Basically, you will become familiar with all the faces in town**, and there will be an understood unity that is found in any small town."

Q "The bookstore is one of the best you will find in the nation. It's a place to study, hang out, and it has anything and everything you would ever want or need. The bookstore has everything and a wonderful staff. Some of the school buildings may have been built close to two centuries ago, but you wouldn't notice it. **Every building is comfortable and well furnished**. I lived in a dorm with carpeting and air-conditioning as a freshman! What more can I ask for. The classrooms are wonderful, and the buildings some of your lectures are in were once homes, and it's just awesome at times when you realize how special of a place Kenyon is. Round-table discussions in almost every class and plenty of opinions to share make up good times!"

Q "**The academic facilities, particularly in the sciences, are excellent**. We have some beautiful classrooms, more historic buildings than you can shake a stick at, and several good performance spaces. The art facilities could use some work, and while there are a few exceptional residences, student housing is fairly primitive. The lack of a student union is not a problem. Gambier's various gathering spaces serve the purpose more than adequately."

Q "The back of the bookstore is an excellent study area. It's also **one of the few places you'll find cute guys** on this campus—I'm serious."

Q "At first, I thought it was kind of weird that we didn't have a student union, but now I can't picture Kenyon with one. We interact so much in our dorms and classes that you don't really need a student union. **The buildings are beautiful, clean, and pretty modern**."

Q "The village is pretty much the equivalent of a student union. Also, **the new gym facility has helped**. The bookstore is a great place to hang out and study. The dorms are very '70s-ish, which I don't like so much. The academic buildings are nice, and Ascension is very classic."

Q "Is Kenyon's lack of a student union a good thing?—No. **Gund Commons is close, although nowhere near adequate**. It's fantastic, although I have a hard time believing the average student goes there seven times a day."

The College Prowler Take On...
Facilities

Kenyon is very proud of the fact that we have no student union. The truth is, we don't need one. The village is built around students, and the campus is not big enough for us to lose track of each other without a central meeting place. Downtown Gambier serves as the center of student life, and the bookstore is the campus heartbeat. Everything from shampoo to staple guns to gummy bears is sold there (books, of course, are too), and there are comfy chairs in every corner. Most buildings on campus are never locked, so there are a plethora of available meeting spaces. The library atrium is one of the most popular, as is the Gund Commons ballroom. Every building on campus is extremely inviting. The majority of the ones on south campus look like castles, and the ones that don't (the library, Ernst) are at least cozy.

Many students are excited about the recently completed $60 million Kenyon Athletic Center, which opened up much-needed space on campus for athletics and offers a gorgeous work-out room. The facility features a pool, tennis court, indoor track, and pro shop. Rosse Hall is the main venue for speakers and large-scale musical performances. Behind it is the smaller Storer Hall, which functions as a rehearsal space for the campus orchestra and a venue for smaller performances. On north campus, Bexley Hall is where the majority of art classes are taught, and the nearby "art barn," containing all sculpture and painting facilities, is where the art majors live during finals time. The Bolton dance studio accommodates the small number of dance majors, and our two theaters are reserved for all plays and drama classes.

B-

The College Prowler® Grade on
Facilities: B-

A high Facilities grade indicates that the campus is aesthetically pleasing and well-maintained; facilities are state-of-the-art, and libraries are exceptional. Other determining factors include the quality of both athletic and student centers and an abundance of things to do on campus.

Campus Dining

The Lowdown On...
Campus Dining

Freshman Meal Plan Requirement?

Yes

Meal Plan Average Cost:

$3,040

Places to Grab a Bite with Your Meal Plan:

Gund Commons

Food: Soup, salad bar, home-style entree, vegetarian options, pasta bar, stir-fry, noodle bar, international entree, grill, pizza station, deli, and desserts

Location: Gund Commons

Hours: Monday–Thursday 7 a.m.–7 p.m., Friday 7 a.m.–1:15 p.m., Sunday 9 a.m.–1 p.m., 5 p.m.–8 p.m.

Philander's Pub

Food: Deli, gourmet pizza

Location: Pierce Hall

Hours: 11:15 a.m.–1:15 p.m.,
5 p.m.–8:30 p.m.

Pierce Hall

Food: Marketplace-style
(soup, pizza, deli, grill,
bakery, home-style, Asian,
Italian, international,
bagels, desserts)

Location: Gund Commons

Hours: Monday–Friday,
7:30 a.m.–7:30 p.m.,
Saturday 8 a.m.–1:15 p.m.,
5 p.m.–7 p.m.

Off-Campus Places to Use Your Meal Plan:

None

24-Hour On-Campus Eating?

None

Students Speak Out On...
Campus Dining

{ **"It's a typical college dining service. Not great, but not disgusting. As far as AVI Foodsystems goes, it was good for the first few weeks, but then it got old."**

Q "Campus dining could be worse and seems to be improving. The dining service managers are extremely receptive to student input and try very hard to provide for everyone and supply us with **a great deal of daily options**. With a little creativity, one can put together decent, healthy meals in the dining halls."

Q "The food is good enough for me. I guess it's good that the food isn't incredible so I don't put on any extra weight, but it's never awful. Sometimes, it's a little repetitive, but there's always a variety of foods to choose from in both Gund and Pierce. **AVI was cool at first, but it's not always great**, and there are always a few pearls offered."

Q "Quality of campus dining? Ha—right! Good joke. It could be worse, I suppose, but for $37,000 a year, it could be a hell of a lot better. **There is a consistent lack of options**. I don't think too many students will fight over that one. As far as AVI, more like Acid Vicious Indigestion. With the exception of the meat carving station, it's Avi Foodsystems with a daily helping of hamburgers."

Q "Surprisingly, I really do love the food here. **I think most college students expect to go out to eat** when they go to the dining hall or something. Kenyon doesn't have tons of options sometimes, but for the most part, it's all really good."

Q "**Dining has really improved**. The 'scramble system' is great if you're not scared of 'cutting' people in line. The pub downstairs offers subs, pizza, and pasta. The all-you-can-eat and extended hours are very convenient."

Q "Gambier itself offers a precious few alternatives to the blandness of Avi Foodsystems. The Gambier Deli makes a pretty good sandwich, but its prices, ($7–$10), make it impossible for them to be a regular part of a student's diet. The Gambier Grill, whose primary function is the campus's only real bar, makes decent grill-type food at an affordable price. **There is also the Kenyon Inn, which serves legitimate three-star gourmet food**, but prices ($40–$50 a head) generally make it an option only when one's parents are in town."

Q "I think that students are always going to complain about food. I think that they are doing a lot to change the food at Kenyon. **They are doing a good job; it is improving**. It is tough because it is such a social point of the day where everyone wants to go to Pierce, and not as many people want to go to Gund anymore, so I think that's a downer, but I think that at the same time, for Kenyon, dinner has always been really important. The longer students feel comfortable going into Pierce or Gund, and finding food that they like and that they can eat, the better. I see it as a great time during the day where I can catch up with my friends that I wouldn't necessarily see elsewhere. You really realize how small and comfortable the size of the student body is when you walk into Pierce, and you can pretty much know you are going to bump into one of your friends."

Q "The 21 meal plan courtesy of Avi Foodsystems is automatically a part of the Kenyon education. The general consensus of the student body is that the quality of the food leaves much to be desired. It is possible to sustain oneself on the food, but **gaining the Freshman 15 from the dining hall food is not a concern**."

Q "Occasionally, a meal, such as chicken patties, will entice the general population's appetites, but those are rare. **Attempts to add flavor to a generally plain menu are often overdone**, and leave it nearing the inedible threshold."

The College Prowler Take On...
Campus Dining

Kenyon is one of the last schools in the country where anyone can simply walk in and eat a meal. This is because we have no meal plan. You go to Pierce, you eat as much as you want for as long as you want. Before you get excited, just remember this plan is born out of desperation, not convenience. If a Kenyon student stops eating in the cafeteria, they are either going to starve or go broke within days. It is not that our food is bad. As college food goes, it is actually pretty decent. The problem at Kenyon lies in familiarity. You will get to know all the campus food options very well, very soon. That is why the school, in conjunction with Avi Foodsystems, the campus food service, recently started an initiative to make the dining experience resemble "real food," as opposed to what students have experienced in the past.

In some ways, it has been successful. Every day, they offer burgers (both beef and veggie), hot dogs, fries, and grilled cheese or chicken patties as an alternative. There is always an entree du jour, usually a meat dish, a pasta dish, and a complimentary vegetable. There is also a salad bar, soup, and cereal at all meals. Pierce Hall has the added bonus of Pangeos, which is various regional dishes (oriental noodles, Mediterranean wraps) cooked up fresh in front of you. The lines for these are usually very long, but it can be well worth your wait. Pierce is where the majority of the upperclassmen eat, and in general, the more popular servery for its options and atmosphere. Gund offers everything above, but is on north campus, and is frequented almost exclusively by non-athletes, freshmen, and north-dwelling upperclassmen. It is more of a "homey" servery, where as Pierce is a little more of a social scene.

B-

The College Prowler® Grade on
Campus Dining: B-

Our grade on Campus Dining addresses the quality of both school-owned dining halls and independent on-campus restaurants as well as the price, availability, and variety of food.

Off-Campus Dining

The Lowdown On...
Off-Campus Dining

Restaurant Prowler:
Popular Places to Eat!

Alcove
Food: Steaks, chops, sandwiches, salads, bar service
116 South Main St., Mt. Vernon
(740) 392-3076
www.alcoverestaurant.com
Price: $6–$16 per person
Hours: Monday–Thursday
11 a.m.–2 p.m., 5 p.m.–
9 p.m., Friday 11 a.m.–2 p.m.,
5 p.m. –9:30 p.m., Saturday
5 p.m.–9:30 p.m.

Bob Evans
Food: American food; breakfast all day
857 Coshocton Ave.
(740) 393-1700
Price: $5–$12 per person
Hours: Daily 6 a.m.–10 p.m.

Fiesta Mexicana
Food: Mexican, bar
308 West High St.
(740) 397-6325
Price: $5–$14 per person

→

(Fiesta Mexicana, continued)
Hours: Monday–Thursday
11 a.m.–2 p.m., 5 p.m.–10 p.m.
Friday–Saturday 12 p.m.–
10 p.m., Sundays 12 p.m.–
9 p.m.

Flappers Bar and Grill
Food: Steaks, chicken, pasta,
sandwiches, bar
15 West High St.
(740) 392-1061
Price: $5–$11 per person
Hours: Monday–Wednesday
11 a.m.–1 a.m., Thursday–
Saturday 11 a.m.–2:30 a.m.

Friendly's Ice Cream Shop
Food: Hamburgers,
sandwiches, ice cream
specialties, breakfasts
803 Coshocton Ave.,
Mt. Vernon
(740) 397-6589
www.friendlys.com
Price: $6–$10 per person
Hours: Daily 7 a.m.–11 p.m.

Gambier Grill & Pizza
Food: Pizza, American
100 E Brooklyn St., Gambier
(740) 427-2200
Price: $6–$8 per person
Hours: Monday, Tuesday,
Thursday 5 p.m.–12:45 a.m.,
Wednesday, Friday, Saturday
5 p.m.–1:45 a.m.

**Henry's at Curtis Inn on
the Square**
Food: American food;
hamburgers, sandwiches,
bar service
12 Public Square, Mt. Vernon
(740) 397-5603
Price: $5–$15 per person
Hours: Monday–Friday
11 a.m.–10 p.m., Saturday
4 p.m.–11 p.m., Sunday
12 p.m.–7 p.m.

Hunan Garden
Food: Hunan and Szechuan
1516 Coshocton Ave.
(740) 393-1313
Price: $6–$13 per person
Hours: Sunday–Thursday
11 a.m.–9 a.m., Friday–
Saturday 11 a.m.–10 p.m.

Jake's Restaurant
Food: American, salads,
steaks, sandwiches
996 Coshocton Ave.
(740) 397-1418
Price: $6–$20 per person
Hours: Sunday–Thursday
11 a.m.–10 p.m., Friday–
Saturday 11 a.m.–11 p.m.

Kenyon Inn
Food: Fine dining
100 W Wiggin St., Gambier
(800) 258-5391
www.kenyoninn.com
Price: $10–$27 per person

(Kenyon Inn, continued)

Hours: Monday–Thursday,
7 a.m.–9 a.m., 11 a.m.–
2 p.m., 5 p.m.–9 p.m., Friday
7 a.m.–9 a.m., 11 a.m.–2 p.m.,
5 p.m.–10 p.m., Saturday
7 a.m.–10 a.m., 11 a.m.–
2 p.m., 5 p.m.–10 p.m., Sunday
10 a.m.–2 p.m., 5 p.m.–9 p.m.

Mazza's Ristorante

Food: Italian, bar

214 W. High St.

(740) 393-2076

Price: $9–$17 per person

Hours: Sunday–Thursday
11 a.m.–10 p.m., Friday
11 a.m.–11 p.m., Saturday
3 p.m.–11 p.m.

Pizza Hut

1061 Coshocton Ave.

Food: Pizza, sandwiches, beer

(740) 397-2275

Price: $4–$16 per person

Hours: Sunday–Thursday
11 a.m.–11 p.m., Friday–
Saturday 11 a.m.–12 a.m.

R&M's Southside Diner

Food: 50s-style diner with
American food and some
Greek specialties

620 S. Main St.

(740) 392-1282

Price: $2–$8 per person

Hours: Monday–Saturday
6 a.m.–8 p.m.,
Sunday 6 a.m.–3 p.m.

Ruby Tuesday

Food: Chicken, hamburgers,
pasta, steaks, salad bar

1055 Coshocton Ave.

(740) 397-3113

www.rubytuesday.com

Price: $6–$14 per person

Hours: Monday–Thursday
11 a.m.–11 p.m., Friday–
Saturday 11 a.m.–12 a.m.,
Sunday 11 a.m.–10 p.m.

Sip's Cafe

Food: Coffee, baked goods,
soups, sandwiches

124 S. Main St.

(740) 392-2233

www.sipscoffeehouse.com

Price: $3–$8 per person

Hours: Monday–Thursday
6:30 a.m.–9 p.m., Friday
6:30 a.m.–11 p.m., Saturday
7:30 a.m.–11 p.m.

Kentucky Fried Chicken

Food: Fried chicken, fast food

301 W. High St.

(740) 392-4900

www.kfc.com

Price: $6–$20 per person

Hours: Daily 10:30 a.m.–9 p.m.

McDonald's

Food: American, fast food

1059 Coshocton Ave.

(740) 397-5503

www.mcdonalds.com

Price: $1–$6 per person

Hours: Open 24 hours

Taco Bell

Food: Mexican fast food
1015 Coshocton Ave.
(740) 393-3133
www.tacobell.com
Price: $2–$6 per person
Hours: Sunday–Thursday
10 a.m.–2 a.m., Friday–
Saturday 10 a.m.–3 a.m.

Wendy's

Food: American, fast food
522 S. Main St.
(740) 397-3440
www.wendys.com
Price: $1–$6 per person
Hours: Daily 10 a.m.–10 p.m.
(drive-thru open until 12 a.m.)

Other Places to Check Out:

Middle Ground Deli (located
on campus, but the meal plan
cannot be used there)
Peggy Sue's Steak & Ribs

Southside Diner

Closest Grocery Store:

Kroger
855 Coshocton Ave.,
Mt Vernon
(740) 393-1425

Best Pizza:

Gambier Grill & Pizza

Best Chinese:

Hunan Garden

Best Breakfast:

R&M's Southside Diner

Best Wings:

Jake's Restaurant

Best Place to Take Your Parents:

Kenyon Inn

Students Speak Out On...
Off-Campus Dining

"There are not so many off-campus dining options close to campus. You either need to have a car or have a friend who has a car to get to any good restaurants. Anything at Easton is good."

Q "There aren't an awful lot of off-campus dining options after 10 or 11 at night. However, there are a few options in Mt. Vernon and, in those cases, you really do need a car. For dinner, you might be able to pick up a sandwich at the deli, but other than that, **it is a little bit harder to find food after 11 o'clock**."

Q "Off-campus options, with a few notable exceptions (the Kenyon Inn, Middle Ground, Deli), are slim—mediocre Mexican, soupy Chinese, fast food, and enough diners to harden the arteries of a 1,500-strong student body with grease left over for the faculty and administration. Fortunately, Kroger is open all night."

Q "**Off-campus dining is pretty limited to crappy food** like Friendly's and McDonald's. The deli on campus is good."

Q "If you go into town, there are enough off-campus dining opportunities, especially if you are married to your favorite fast food chain. If not, it's basically Ruby Tuesday, Jake's, the Alcove, and Fiesta. **Jake's and the Alcove are the best**. Jake's is like Applebee's (or a similar chain), whereas the Alcove probably touches $20/meal including drinks, excluding dessert."

Q "Mt. Vernon has several options for food, and there are some relative roses among the thorns of fast food. The most popular is a restaurant called Jake's, which serves quality **American-style food, with a pleasant atmosphere** for a very reasonable price."

Q "About a 20-minute drive from Gambier is Peggy Sue's, which is a little known but **very good home-style restaurant** where one can get a big meal for $10."

The College Prowler Take On...
Off-Campus Dining

Because your meal plan only covers the three dining halls, everything else, regardless of location, will be considered off-campus. The best option for local dining is the Gambier Grill & Pizza. It offers very good pizza and other Italian options. The typical meal there will cost somewhere around $8, though, which can be a little pricey for a student's budget. The Gambier Grill offers burgers, chicken wings, and the like, but the food is eaten mostly as late-night delivery. The Grill's main function is as the campus bar. The Middle Ground serves as a coffee and lunch spot, and is a pleasant alternative to what Avi Foodsystems has to offer. The best local dining is at the Kenyon Inn, but at $50 a head, it is usually seen only during parental visits and very special occasions. The Kenyon Inn is the only place in Gambier that you will ever see a tablecloth.

For those with a car, the real dining options are in Mt. Vernon—if it's cheap, or a chain, it's in Vernon. There is fast food, such as McDonalds, Wendy's, Taco Bell, and KFC, and then there are the chains, such as Friendly's, Bob Evans, Ruby Tuesday. There are several restaurants in Mount Vernon that fall into neither of these categories, and they are actually quite good. Jake's is a place for steak, and can be a little expensive when ordering its feature item, but also has great burgers at a much lower price. The Southside diner serves breakfast all day. Hunan Garden, probably the most frequented of the non-chain restaurants, is also the best. It serves Chinese food and should not be missed.

The College Prowler® Grade on
Off-Campus Dining: C

A high Off-Campus Dining grade implies that off-campus restaurants are affordable, accessible, and worth visiting. Other factors include the variety of cuisine and the availability of alternative options (vegetarian, vegan, Kosher, etc.).

Campus Housing

The Lowdown On...
Campus Housing

Room Types:
Standard doubles, triples, or even some singles share bathrooms on floor or wing

Suite style – a set of rooms adjoined by a common room

Private – private bathrooms or share with one other person

Apartment – suite-style rooms with a shared bathroom per apartment

Best Dorms:
Manning, Tafts

Worst Dorms:
Caples, Leonard

Number of Dormitories:
13

Number of University-Owned Apartments:
4

Undergrads Living on Campus:
98%

Dormitories:

Bushnell Hall

Floors: 2 plus basement

Total Occupancy: 51

Bathrooms: Two per wing

Coed: No, all women

Residents: Upperclassmen

Room Types: Standard doubles

Special Features: Large main lounge with TV and cable, kitchen in basement, carpeted hallway, window blinds, moveable furniture, large student storage room.

Caples Residence Hall

Floors: 9 plus basement

Total Occupancy: 146

Bathrooms: Two per floor

Coed: Yes

Residents: Upperclassmen

Room Types: Standard singles, doubles, and suites (6-person, 2-person)

Special Features: Kitchen on first-floor, handicapped accessible, TV lounge with cable, laundry facility in basement, fully carpeted rooms and hallways, limited furniture provided in suite lounges, adjustable heating and air-conditioning, movable furniture, venetian blinds, limited furniture provided in suite lounges, poor lighting in suites, suite doubles are small, and rooms around trash chute and elevator can be noisy.

Farr Hall

Floors: 1

Total Occupancy: 34

Bathrooms: Singles share adjoining bathroom, doubles have private bathroom

Coed: Yes

Residents: Upperclassmen

Room Types: Double, single, suites, apartment

Special Features: Cable availability, laundry facilities, fully carpeted, two-person apartments have bathroom and kitchenette (includes two-burner stove, sink, refrigerator), but building can be noisy from street traffic, no air-conditioning, and no common lounge.

Gund Hall

Floors: 2 plus basement

Total Occupancy: 81

Bathrooms: One per wing

Coed: Yes, single sex floors

Residents: Freshmen

Room Types: Standard

Special Features: Venetian blinds, large lounge with television, laundry facility in basement, study lounges on each floor, exercise facility, built-in room dividers (featuring a bookshelf and bulletin board, built in furniture and storage compartments).

Hanna Hall

Floors: 3 plus basement

Total Occupancy: 78

Bathrooms: Four per floor

Coed: Yes

Residents: Upperclassmen

Room Types: Standard doubles and triples

Special Features: Large rooms, large windows with venetian blinds, fully carpeted rooms and hallways, lounges include TV with cable, but wardrobes are attached to the walls and not movable.

Leonard Hall

Floors: 4 plus basement

Total Occupancy: 93

Bathrooms: Two per floor

Coed: Yes

Residents: Upperclassmen

Room Types: Standard singles, doubles, and triples

Special Features: Bay window, several windows in doubles, rooms and hallway carpeted, large doubles, lounges with cable TV, but there are few bathrooms and wardrobes are attached to walls.

Lewis Hall

Floors: 2

Total Occupancy: 83

Bathrooms: One per wing

Coed: Yes

Residents: Freshmen

Room Types: Standard

(Lewis Hall, continued)

Special Features: Recently remodeled, new furniture, rooms have large windows, built in wardrobes, lounge with cable TV, microwave oven and vending machine, laundry.

Manning Hall

Floors: 2 plus basement

Total Occupancy: 51

Bathrooms: Two per wing

Coed: Yes

Residents: Upperclassmen

Room Types: Standard doubles

Special Features: Movable furniture, venetian blinds, laundry facility, kitchen area on first floor, large TV lounge with cable, Ping-Pong table, study lounge with Internet ports in basement, study lounge with Internet ports in basement, carpeted hallways.

Mather Hall

Floors: 4 plus basement

Total Occupancy: 177

Bathrooms: Two per floor

Coed: Yes, Single sex by room

Residents: Freshmen (first floor only) and upperclassmen

Room Types: Standard singles, doubles, triples

Special Features: Venetian blinds, laundry facility in basement, kitchen area, fully carpeted, large TV lounge with cable, adjustable heating and air-conditioning.

(Mather Hall, continued)

vending machines, large central kitchen, and computer lab, but shower heads are low, poor lighting, and furniture is not moveable.

McBride Hall

Floors: 3 plus basement

Total Occupancy: 184

Bathrooms: Two per floor

Coed: Yes, single-sex by room

Residents: Freshmen

Room Types: Standard

Special Features: Movable furniture, venetian blinds, laundry facility in basement, kitchen area, fully carpeted, large TV lounge with cable, adjustable heating and air-conditioning, vending machines, computer room, and large central kitchen.

Norton Hall

Floors: 2

Total Occupancy: 78

Bathrooms: One per wing

Coed: Yes

Residents: Freshmen

Room Types: Standard

Special Features: Venetian blinds with recessed curtain rods, movable furniture, built-in wardrobes, lounge with cable TV, microwave oven, vending machine, well heated but usually hot in the winter, laundry facilities.

Old Kenyon Hall

Floors: 4 plus basement

Total Occupancy: 144

Bathrooms: Two per floor

Coed: Yes

Residents: Upperclassmen

Room Types: Standard single, double, triple

Special Features: Movable furniture, venetian blinds, laundry facility in basement, microwave in basement, four large TV lounges in basement, patios, study lounge with table in basement, fully carpeted rooms and hallways, student storage on fourth floor, but noise level can be high, concrete walls, and wardrobes are attached to wall.

Watson Hall

Floors: 2 plus basement

Total Occupancy: 43

Bathrooms: One per floor

Coed: Yes

Residents: Upperclassmen

Room Types: Standard singles and doubles

Special Features: Movable furniture, venetian blinds, laundry facility in basement, kitchen on first floor, carpeted hallways, large TV lounge with cable, built in wardrobes, adjacent parking lot quietest dorm, but only small bookcases available.

Campus Apartments:

Acland Apartments

Total Occupancy: 48

Bathrooms: One bathroom in each six-person apartment

Coed: Yes, single sex by apartment

Residents: Upperclassmen

Room Types: Standard doubles

Special Features: Very large common room, stove, oven, small refrigerator, but no air-conditioning.

Bexley Apartments

Total Occupancy: 55

Bathrooms: One per each three- or four-person apartment

Coed: Yes, single-sex by apartment

Residents: Upperclassmen

Room Types: Standard singles

Special Features: Air-conditioning, kitchenette (with small refrigerator, sink, microwave), large living room (including TV hookup and cable availability, sofa, coffee table and other furniture provided), adjacent parking lot, but no trash pick-up at individual apartment (pick-up only at main trash facility).

New Apartments

Total Occupancy: 150

Bathrooms: Large bathroom in each apartment

Coed: Yes, single sex by apartment

Residents: Upperclassmen

Room Types: Standard

Special Features: Air-conditioning, kitchenette (with small refrigerator, sink, stovetop burners), large living room (including TV hookup and cable availability, sofa, coffee table and other furniture provided), adjacent parking lot, but kitchenette is part of living room, can be noisy between rooms, poor lighting, no trash pick-up at individual apartment (pick-up only at main trash facility).

Taft Cottages

Total Occupancy: 48

Bathrooms: One per each four-person apartment

Coed: Yes, single sex by apartment

Residents: Upperclassmen

Room Types: Standard

Special Features: Air conditioned, kitchenette (with small refrigerator, sink, microwave), large living room (including TV hookup and cable availability, sofa, coffee table and other furniture provided), large windows, laundry facility in building, a window seats on second floor, cathedral ceilings on third floor.

Housing Offered:

Singles: 27%

Doubles: 37%

Triples/Suites: 3%

Apartments: 23%

Bed Type

36"x 80"extra-long twin

Cleaning Service?

Residence hall bathrooms are cleaned daily; apartment bathrooms are cleaned once a week.

You Get

Students in dorms recieve a single bed, desk (28"x 40") and chair, bureau with five drawers, closet with sliding doors or a half dresser with four drawers and half wardrobe with storage cabinets above, wastebasket, and several permanent light fixtures (located on room ceiling or above the desk, mirror, and/or bed, depending on dorm). Students in apartments also receive a furnished kitchen or kitchenette and living room.

Students Speak Out On...
Campus Housing

"Housing is okay. Bexley, New Apartments, and Aclands, which are upperclass housing, are a lot nicer than the dorms, which are very antiquated."

Q "I've never been unhappy with anywhere I've lived at Kenyon. **Every year, I feel like I've always been given a good room**, and I think that, for the most part, all of the dorms are pretty nice. Obviously, some are nicer than others, but we don't have any real high rises, we have one high rise building on campus, but I think we are lucky that the majority of our dorms are not more than two stories high."

Q "There is a range of on-campus housing. We have a few beautiful dorms, mostly doubles and triples, with a few singles, which are populated primarily by frat boys and party kids. **The freshman housing is grim**, but fosters a real sense of community. By the time you get to be a junior and senior, it's possible to get an on-campus apartment, some of which are stunningly beautiful, and some of which are pretty ramshackle; we get by."

Q "No matter how nice your dorm is, **it will feel like a dungeon by the end of the first month**. There are many methods to counteract this. For instance, do your homework somewhere else. Walk outside, and in the typical freshman fashion, gawk at the image of Pierce Tower against the stars. To be content on this campus, you need to appreciate quiet beauty, such as walking through fields. It helps to have a friend with a car."

Q "Most of the on-campus housing offered is clean and comfortable, but **there aren't nearly enough singles on campus**. A small, close community like Kenyon can be a wonderful place to spend four years, but in order to thrive in such a tight-knit environment, personal space is so important. Especially for juniors and seniors, who are really becoming adults, being forced to live with roommates for four years can be stifling."

Q "The rooms in the freshman quad are huge. These are some of the biggest I've been in anywhere, and I did a lot of college touring. **The dorms are all really nice** if you want to make them nice. The windows are big, and there's lots of wall space to decorate and such."

Q "Some at Kenyon feel that some of the money spent on the FRA should have gone to building new dorms. While there are some nice dorms that might score an eight out of ten, far too many students, especially sophomores, **feel there is definite room for improvement**."

Q "If you wanted to get an accurate view of Kenyon's dorms, you need only look at the ones designated for freshmen. First, there are Norton and Lewis, which are known as the historics. **Externally beautiful with spacious rooms**, these dorms are generally the preferred ones, despite the absence of amenities such as air-conditioning and carpeting, which are featured in McBride and Mather."

Q "Caples, an upperclass dorm, is a nine-story pencil, and it is generally considered **the least desirable dorm on campus**."

Q "The lack of off-campus housing **enhances the sense of community**. I love living on campus."

The College Prowler Take On...
Campus Housing

In the interest of maintaining a community, Kenyon maintains a strict residential campus. Most students live on campus all four years, and in these times, the dorms function as centers of non-academic student life. Kenyon housing can be evenly divided into two categories—dorms and apartments. Freshmen all live in dorms, and they live in the same area of campus. Lewis, Norton, and Gund make up the freshmen quad. These dorms are large, and the architecture resembles that of the historic buildings of south campus. Across the street are Mather and McBride, the former housing a few freshmen, as well. These rooms are slightly smaller, but they are air conditioned, and their separation fosters its own tight-knit community. There are a fair number of available singles in these dorms, and a doctor's note is the surest way to get one.

The other options for housing at Kenyon are in one of the many on-campus apartments. There are three-, four- and six-person apartments available. Many juniors and seniors live the apartment life. Some of the most desirable of the upperclass apartments are the Bexley Apartments, where every inhabitant gets a single. Farr Hall, which is in the exact center of campus— above the bookstore—features bathrooms and kitchens. South campus has its Taft Cottages, which actually look like very nice real-world apartments, and give the Bexley's a run for their money. They are the newest buildings on campus, unlike the "New" Apartments, which have been around for decades. The last apartment option is the Aclands. They are located in the middle of campus and have their own parking, but are slightly dilapidated. The enormous common rooms enhance the overall appeal, but also lend themselves to a great many parties. These are fun for the owner of the apartment, but can be less fun for the surrounding neighbors.

The College Prowler® Grade on
Campus Housing: B-

A high Campus Housing grade indicates that dorms are clean, well-maintained, and spacious. Other determining factors include variety of dorms, proximity to classes, and social atmosphere.

Off-Campus Housing

The Lowdown On...
Off-Campus Housing

Undergrads in Off-Campus Housing:

2%

Average Rent For:

1 BR Apt.: $350–$450/mo.

2 BR Apt.: $510–$715/mo.

3 BR Apt.: $609–$875/mo.

About Off-Campus Housing:

Students who would like to live off campus must request to do so, and permission must then be granted. However, off-campus housing sometimes becomes necessary when there is not enough space for students in campus housing.

Students Speak Out On...
Off-Campus Housing

"An increasingly popular trend for those left in the cold by the lottery is to find an underclassman willing to pay both shares in a double in exchange for the senior living in a vacancy in an off-campus apartment."

Q "I absolutely love the fact that there is barely any off-campus housing. It unifies the campus. I visited a larger university in Atlanta, and most sophomores lived off campus and had to commute to class. Part of Kenyon's magic is walking by the same people on the Middle Path and eventually stopping and saying 'Hey, I see you all the time. What's your name?' And you make a friend. That wouldn't happen if people lived off campus."

Q "Off-campus housing is decidedly inconvenient, since almost all activities are based on campus."

Q "In order to live off campus, you can enter the housing lottery, be assigned to a room, and then choose to live in an apartment and pay both the Kenyon boarding fee and the apartment rent, or you can be approved for off-campus housing by the Office of Residential Life, have your Kenyon boarding fee waived, and pay rent for an apartment. Either way, it's much more expensive than living on campus (rent is more than the Kenyon boarding fee), and the few off-campus options that exist aren't terribly different from many of the Kenyon housing options. Despite all this, it's tempting to live off campus just to know a bit more responsibility and freedom."

The College Prowler Take On...
Off-Campus Housing

We don't have very many students that live off campus. There are usually around 15 people that live off campus, but they undergo the very selective application process. Kenyon strongly believes in its community, and as a result, everyone lives together on campus. The only exceptions to this stringent rule are a slightly larger percentage of students who live in apartments that are designated "off-campus" by about 20 yards. The "Milk Carton" apartments are visible from the dining hall and throw a lot of parties in warm weather. Each milk carton seems to correspond to a specific frat, sport, or visible social clique, so you can usually determine the crowd of a party just by knowing the apartment number. The "Pizza Hut" apartments are slightly farther away, and look like low-rise city project housing.

One other thing to know about these apartments is that nobody is living there by school permission, so students can be very creative in how they live there. The most popular trick is to apply for a double on campus and not live in it. That way, you get your apartment and the other person gets a double single. This is a fairly common practice, and results in a lot of students with double singles.

The College Prowler® Grade on

Off-Campus Housing: D-

A high grade in Off-Campus Housing indicates that apartments are of high quality, close to campus, affordable, and easy to secure.

Diversity

The Lowdown On...
Diversity

Native American:
Less than 1%

White:
88%

Asian American:
3%

International:
3%

African American:
3%

Out-of-State:
78%

Hispanic:
2%

Political Activity

Many Kenyon students have outspoken political beliefs, and all student e-mail account, allstus, is a popular forum for political debate. Rallies or demonstrations are few and far between, but they do occur.

Gay Pride

Most students at Kenyon are fairly accepting in terms of homosexuality. There have been isolated incidents of insensitivity, but they do not represent the opinion of the campus as a whole. The school recently opened a unity house to serve as a community center and safe space for the GLBTQQA community.

Most Popular Religions

The school was founded as Episcopalian, and although the tie between Kenyon and church is almost nonexistent, Christians are still the biggest group on campus, however, there seems to be adequate Jewish representation, as well.

Economic Status

The typical Kenyon is the product of a suburban upbringing and a private school, thus many of the students come from upper-middle-class backgrounds, but there are plenty of exceptions to the rule.

Minority Clubs

Adelante, ALSO (Allied Sexual Orientation), ASIA (Asian students for international awareness), ISAK (International Students at Kenyon).

Students Speak Out On...
Diversity

"There's a lack of diversity, and it is noticeable, but Kenyon does have the most diverse group of upper-middle-class white students. Also, Kenyon is working on improving racial diversity, as well as sexual diversity."

Q "Is its lack at Kenyon noticeable? Yes. Kenyon's lack of diversity is noticeable, but **not as bad as one would think**. When I applied to schools, diversity was something I looked at, mainly because it seems pompous and borderline discriminatory not to look, but when it boils down to it, it's not that big of a deal."

Q "Kenyon's diversity is not lacking in any means. **Everyone is so different**, it's incredible. If you base diversity on skin color, yes, Kenyon lacks diversity in race, but in every other aspect—religion, lifestyle, economic background, and life experiences—each person is fascinating."

Q "I would say that at Kenyon, you have a very diverse group of white, upper-middle-class students. Kenyon has a fairly large amount of international students, but there aren't a lot of African American students that are attracted to Kenyon. I think that the **Admissions Office works very hard to find African American applicants**, but it hasn't really gotten to the point where Kenyon is as diverse as it could be. Maybe that has to do with its location being in Ohio."

Q "It takes a certain type of student to go to college in really what is the middle-of-nowhere in Ohio. It is a great school, and there is a lot that it offers, but for a lot of people, they really are forced to make their own fun during the week and weekends. Therefore, you have **a lot of very independently-minded students**."

Q "There are people literally from all over the world and all 50 states. **There is every religion** and ethnic group you could imagine."

Q "I have definitely met a lot of people from different states and different countries. There are also a lot of religions on campus, and **a lot of religious activities**, so if you are religious at all, or just want to meet people in the same religion, there are a lot of opportunities for that."

Q "I came from an almost all-white high school, and it was great to be surrounded by all ethnicities and backgrounds. It is such a **wonderful cultural experience**."

Q "Culturally, Kenyon College is very diverse. Overseas, it is an extremely popular university to attend, so it **attracts students from many continents** and countries around the world. Chances are, you will have several international students in every class, which provides for a much more dynamic and culturally-relevant discussion of the subjects."

The College Prowler Take On...
Diversity

Kenyon is a small, expensive school in a remote location, and as a result, attracts a very specific type of student. A portrait of a typical Kenyon student is white and fairly affluent. While the school is having some success in racially diversifying the campus, racial minorities are still rare. Efforts to add some socioeconomic diversity seem to have faired slightly better, bringing a different perspective to the school.

Diversity expands to looking at other students' backgrounds, and in that respect, Kenyon is diverse. If one's definition of diversity is based on skin color, then Kenyon is not very diverse. When looking at diversity, one has to look beyond skin color or ethnic background, and look at things such as religion, economic background, and where students are from geographically. There are quite a bit of students who are not only from different states in the United States, but also are from different countries. A quarter of Kenyon students are from Ohio, but geographic diversity is increasing. The school is gaining a better reputation on the coast, attracting many from both New York and California. Washington DC and Maryland both have spectacular showings at Kenyon, and non-Ohio Midwesterners, most notably from the Chicago area, are increasing their numbers.

D+

The College Prowler® Grade on

Diversity: D+

A high grade in Diversity indicates that ethnic minorities and international students have a notable presence on campus and that students of different economic backgrounds, religious beliefs, and sexual preferences are well-represented.

Guys & Girls

The Lowdown On...
Guys & Girls

Men Undergrads:
47%

Women Undergrads:
53%

Birth Control Available?
Yes

Hookups or Relationships?
Kenyon's location pretty much narrows the dating options
down to "meet you in the cafeteria" and "let's take a walk,"
so people here are usually either just hooking up or practically
married. Kenyon's incestuously small enrollment leaves little
room for middle ground.

Social Scene

There are two distinct breeds of parties on campus. The first is the dimly-lit, tightly-packed, multi-keg, booty-dancing, and singing-along-to-classic-rock party. These usually take place in dorm lounges or fraternity lodges, and are a great way to simply cut loose on a weekend night. Their beer lines are long, however, the atmosphere is not very conducive to actual conversation, and students often become disillusioned with the whole scene as they get older. These parties are most fun if you either are really drunk or very fond of dancing. Those who don't find either criteria appealing usually stick to the apartment scene. Juniors and seniors living in college apartments will often throw smaller parties. An apartment party can run the gamut from several friends hanging out to floor-sagging ragers, but usually, they fall somewhere in the middle. There are several distinct advantages to this scene. The first is that you are actually able to talk to someone without screaming in his or her ear. It is often easier to find a drink in these situations, and they often go on much later than the registered lounge parties, which are broken up at 2 a.m. by security.

Every year, Kenyon pays for two school-wide parties. The first, Philanders Phling, happens in February and is designed to help students get through the long, Ohio winter. It is a formal, thrown in Pierce Hall, and seemingly the entire campus shows up (drunk) and in their Sunday best. While it can be a blast, many first-years complain that it is reminiscent of prom, where the enormous buildup of the event leads to disappointment upon arrival. Also like prom, many students miss it by getting too drunk too soon, so caution is advised in that area. The second of these parties, Summer Sendoff, is thrown in May, on the last weekend before finals. The drinking starts early in the morning and continues throughout the day at many informal barbeques and open rooms. The day is capped by a concert from a fairly famous band, and the drinking continues as long as the students can keep their eyes open, an ability usually lost around midnight. For many, Summer Sendoff is the highlight of the year.

Best Place to Meet Guys/Girls

At the beginning of freshman year, much of the coupling happens within halls. Dorms are the first fully-constructed social unit a freshman encounters, and as a result, many decide to conduct their romantic affairs in-house. "Dorm-cest" usually leads down one of two roads. Some people graduate with boyfriends/girlfriends they've had since swimming pre-season four years prior, and some realize that the incredibly short walk-of-shame isn't worth seeing your hookup every morning when you're brushing your teeth.

After that, Kenyon is so small and personable that virtually any populated campus location can serve as a singles bar. The bookstore, the library, even the servery line are all perfectly viable locations to strike up a conversation with someone you've had your eye on. Striking up a conversation with a stranger is very easy to do. Comments on the class you have together or the length of the cafeteria line can easily lead to friendships, dates, and who knows what else.

If you're the less patient type, immediate gratification can most easily be found at a frat party. Kenyon people are very friendly as it is, so putting 100 or so drunk ones in a room together, combined with low-lighting and booty music, can lead to a lot of interesting situations.

Did You Know?

Top Three Places to Find Hotties:
1. The Library (it's a bar without alcohol)
2. Frat parties (if that's your scene)
3. Denison University (sad but true)

Top Five Places to Hook Up:
1. Mather laundry room
2. Weaver Cottage
3. The library atrium
4. Someone else's room
5. The art barn

Dress Code

Looking around a Kenyon cafeteria, a newcomer would see a very confusing pastiche of styles. At a given table, you could see a girl wearing a J.Crew tank top talking to a guy in a full sweatsuit who is sitting next to someone wearing a top hat and a cape.

Though it may seem confusing at first, Kenyon students' dress habits can be broken up into three distinct cycles, no matter what their personal style is. The daytime mode of dress is typical collegiate casual. You will see people in classes or at lunch wearing sweatpants, T-shirts, fleeces, and the like. This usually lasts until dinner time, when the slightly more presentable clothes are put on to match the social scene in Pierce dining hall or Olin Library. This is the time when students put in immense amounts of effort to look like they got dressed effortlessly. The third style of dressing, party night, finds every social group dressed in their typical fashion, but more so. Preppy guys put on button-ups, and the hipsters find their favorite thrift store T-shirts. If necessary, a student could make it through their four years here without ever donning a tie or dress. There is the occasional semi-formal, usually thrown by the frats, but if you arrive late enough, no one cares what you wear.

In general, the Kenyon rule seems to be "look decent." You don't walk around the bookstore at night in mesh shorts and a muscle shirt (though it happens), but if you put in a slight effort, no one is going to call you a slob.

Students Speak Out On...
Guys & Girls

"Relationship-wise, you find that there is no middle ground or very little middle ground. Some couples are very, very close and tight, almost married, to just occasional hookups, but you'll probably find that everywhere."

Q "**People either get engaged or hook up**. There's nothing in between. There are a lot of attractive people, but most of them are engaged."

Q "It is about a half-and-half split between hookups, friends with benefits, and really intense relationships. **There's a good range of attractiveness on campus**."

Q "Everyone is different, but I think that since you will be living with the same people for four years, **some people are intimidated** by the fact of hooking up and having relationships early in their Kenyon career."

Q "For any teenage male, anything with two legs usually attracts attention. If physical beauty is your thing, yes, you'll find it at Kenyon, as well as the true beauty of a person—their personality. **Girls dress really nice**, so I can't wait until spring and warm weather."

Q "**Kenyon is a very good-looking campus** with all sorts of types—it just depends on what you're looking for. But yes, as a girl, for the most part, the guys are definitely more attractive than guys I've seen at other schools."

Q "In terms of relationships on campus, I'd say the campus is pretty divided. There are those who want random hookups, but as time goes on, often you hear stories from the same individuals over and over, and realize it's more of a 'hookup circle.' The people who want relationships are often harder to find, but are there. In terms of how 'hot' the student body is, there are 'hot' people, and then there are those who don't classify people as hot or not. Whichever you are, you'll find your clique, and if it's hot people you want, you'll find them. **It will help if you are a guy because the guy/girl ratio favors you**."

Q "**Most people I know have found long-term relationships**, but the general consensus on whether guys and girls are hot seems to be a resounding 'no' on both accounts."

Q "Most of the people in my dorm go for casual hookups, but then **we're the 'party' freshman dorm**, so I don't know how universal that is."

The College Prowler Take On...
Guys & Girls

After a little time at Kenyon, you will become very familiar with a little thing called "the Kenyon goggles." This is a phenomenon that allows average looking men and women to be thought of as extremely hot by the rest of the student body. Why? For a school once rated as one of the country's most promiscuous, our general student body is not always easy on the eye. There are a great many cuties, but genuine hotties run few and far between. As a result, ordinary and slightly-above-average looking people find it extremely easy to find dates and hookups, and even the most unlikely student can find someone they really like. The good news is that we are improving. While many still feel that Kenyon guys are better looking than Kenyon girls, each incoming class brings in its notable additions, and the general looks of things are improving.

Once you decide exactly who you have your eye on, you may discover that someone you know has already done, dated, and/or dumped this person. It is not that we are overly promiscuous, but dating tends to happen within certain social circles. Certain guys have been known to tear through particular female groups of friends and vice versa. There is also the strong incestuous vibe that comes with being in such a close community. Everyone knows everybody else's business, and it is hard to meet someone with a clean slate if you have any kind of history on campus. For that reason, there is not a whole lot of dating. There is a lot of hooking up, and a lot of serious couples, but there are not a whole lot of people in the process of getting to know each other. If both parties go to Kenyon, chances are, they already know each other.

The College Prowler® Grade on
Guys: B-

A high grade for Guys indicates that the male population on campus is attractive, smart, friendly, and engaging, and that the school has a decent ratio of guys to girls.

The College Prowler® Grade on
Girls: C+

A high grade for Girls not only implies that the women on campus are attractive, smart, friendly, and engaging, but also that there is a fair ratio of girls to guys.

Athletics

The Lowdown On...
Athletics

Athletic Division:
NCAA Division III

Conference:
NCAC

School Mascot:
Lords and Ladies

**Males Playing
Varsity Sports:**
214 (30%)

**Females Playing
Varsity Sports:**
175 (21%)

➜

Men's Varsity Sports:

Baseball

Basketball

Cross-Country

Football

Golf

Lacrosse

Soccer

Swimming

Tennis

Track & Field (Indoor and Outdoor)

Women's Varsity Sports:

Basketball

Cross-Country

Field Hockey

Lacrosse

Soccer

Softball

Swimming

Tennis

Track & Field (Indoor and Outdoor)

Volleyball

Club Sports:

Archery

Soccer

Cycling

Equestrian

Fencing

Ice Hockey

Juggling

Kickboxing

Lawnsports Society

Martial Arts

Outing

Rugby (Men's and Women's)

Sand Volleyball

Squash

Ultimate Frisbee (Men's and Women's)

Intramurals:

Basketball

Dodgeball

Flag Football

Hockey

Soccer

Volleyball

Athletic Fields

Mavec Field, McBride Feld, McCloskey Field

Getting Tickets

Tickets are free to students, and some games at McBride Field may be $1.

Most Popular Sports

Lacrosse, basketball

Overlooked Teams

Cross-country, swimming, tennis

Best Place to Take a Walk

The Kokosing Gap trail is an Ohio landmark that begins in Gambier.

Gyms/Facilities

Ernst Center

The Ernst Center is located within the Kenyon Athletic Center. It has a nice gym and a pool, which although primarily used for varsity teams, also is available at certain times for non-athletes.

The Temporary Fieldhouse

The Temp is essentially a practice gym for many of the out of season teams. It has a large surface that can be two basketball courts. It also has a small weight area with free weights and a few machines.

The Kenyon Athletic Center

The brand new athletic center offers a multi-activity court, a recreational gym, indoor track, pool and spa, wet classroom (available by reservation only and with lifeguard on duty), tennis courts, four indoor courts, Tomsich basketball arena (reserved for varsity team practice and contests), locker rooms, steam and dry saunas, team training area, conference rooms (including multimedia equipment), weight and fitness room, two multipurpose rooms with mirrored walls and sound equipment, a theater that seats 120 people, four racquetball courts, and eight squash courts.

Students Speak Out On...
Athletics

{ **"Football's not too big here. IM sports are a popular way to have fun and carry on playing sports if you're not too serious about them."**

Q "**Kenyon is definitely not a jock school**. The typical Kenyon student is very intellectual and very interested in classes; a lot of people talk about their classes outside of the classroom. Everyone seems to think pretty strongly about everything that goes on at Kenyon. They are very conscious of the community around them, and athletics are important, but there is definitely not that much of an emphasis put on them."

Q "We excel at geeky, patrician sports like swimming, and are laughably bad at jock sports like football. With that said, **a huge number of people here are active and athletic** without being jocks. Intramural sports are popular and a lot of fun."

Q "IM sports are a presence at Kenyon, drawing perhaps an additional 20 percent of students to athletics, primarily **through soccer, football, and basketball leagues**."

Q "In terms of quantity of sports, Kenyon **matches up well with any other Division III, liberal-arts school**. Quality, however, is at best another matter entirely. While there are some successful programs, the majority of Kenyon teams are mediocre."

Q "As to the athletic scene, **intramural women's rugby is decidedly the optimal sport on campus**. Anyone can play; the captains are willing to teach you. There are no coaches, just other girls. It's a great way to stay in shape, get out aggression, and feel unconventional. It also guarantees you a safe and song-filled social life— c'mon now!"

Q "Kenyon is not a jock school, although I see it rapidly getting there, with the addition of FRA. At the same time, we needed a new facility desperately, and this will most definitely attract student athletes. I don't want to see it move towards a division in the student body as a cross-country runner. I enjoy the fact that **I can be a student, a singer, a writer, and an athlete** without feeling the need to restrict myself. Sports are moderately important to students, and not so much to the community, with the exception of swimming, which I wouldn't consider a jock sport. I think swimming and football get the most attention, for opposite reasons. In addition, the 'game-oriented' sports, such as soccer and field hockey, get the most attention. Due to the nature of the sport, XC is overlooked, and golf is nonexistent, but understandably so."

Q "I feel like a **majority of the students do play sports here**, but I don't get the sense that it's a jock school. And if you don't play a sport, you're definitely not looked down upon."

Q "The two highest profile sports are football and men's basketball. Football, which has heightened importance because of Kenyon's location in Ohio, and men's basketball has had three coaches in the past six years, regularly only draw 300 to 400 people to a weekend game. Those numbers put us **near the bottom of our conference**."

The College Prowler Take On...
Athletics

On a campus comprised of many talented writers, artists, and scientists, sports simply do not occupy a significant spot on the Kenyon student's agenda. Football games are perhaps the most attended sport, followed closely by basketball games in the winter; however, a Saturday afternoon game will draw only a couple hundred students. The non-athletic student body is also not enticed by the reputation of Kenyon sports, especially in the recent past. The exception that laps the rule, quite literally, are the swim Lords and Ladies. Kenyon's swimming teams have built themselves into a powerhouse for nearly the last quarter century. They have reined over Division III, and regularly recruit Division I-caliber athletes. Overall, the Lords have a total of 56 conference championships to their name, and the women have won 20 in 21 years. Kenyon has become nationally renowned as a school for "swimming and English." The thought that the swimmers will win has taken its place next to the English major being on the breadlines after graduation as a campus-wide assumption.

About 15 to 20 percent of the school tries to recapture their high school glory by playing in one of the IM leagues. Though these games don't draw huge audiences, the team members like to create rabid inter-league rivalries that will occasionally spill over into other realms of Kenyon life. Trash talk can spread to the dorms, cafeterias, and e-mail accounts until the rest of the campus will be forced to respond, even if it is to merely say "shut up."

The College Prowler® Grade on
Athletics: C-

A high grade in Athletics indicates that students have school spirit, that sports programs are respected, that games are well-attended, and that intramurals are a prominent part of student life.

Nightlife

The Lowdown On...
Nightlife

Club and Bar Prowler:
Popular Nightlife Spots!

Banana Joe's
100 W High St., Mount Vernon
(740) 392-7400

Banana Joe's is a local club—almost. The bar features a happy hour on Fridays, a karaoke night, and a dance floor. Even so, Banana Joe's is usually an older hang-out, and Kenyon students usually tire of the scene pretty quickly.

Fiesta Mexicana
308 W High St.
(740) 397-6325

Fiesta's offers beer and margaritas, and that's about it—they're mostly a food service establishment, but the bar does get busy on weekend nights.

➔

Flappers Bar and Grill

15 W High St.

(740) 392-1061

Flappers is both a bar and restaurant. Students who love live music flock here to catch local and cover bands.

Gambier Grill & Pizza

100 E Brooklyn St., Gambier

(740) 427-2200

Gambier Grill is an on-campus restaurant and bar where students cannot use their meal plans, but that doesn't stop them from spending all of their free time (or free cash) there. This is probably the biggest Kenyon hangout, as far as the bar scene goes.

Favorite Drinking Games:

Beer Pong

Card Games

Never Have I Ever

Power Hour

Quarters

Roxanne

What to Do if You're Not 21

Because of Kenyon's location, what to do under or over 21 is limited to mostly on-campus activities. There are always events being held, parties to attend, or sporting events to participate in or go see.

Frats

See the Greek section!

Students Speak Out On...
Nightlife

{ "I'm always busy with parties, clubs, girls, or whatever. We find stuff to do."

Q "There are a lot of options for nightlife at Kenyon—as many as you can expect at a small school. You hear very few complaints about there being things to do. A lot of people, if there isn't something to do, will create fun for themselves. I think that is one of the greatest skills you can learn coming out of Kenyon. You really won't have things arranged or planned for you. **People are forced to become very independent and create fun for themselves**, whatever that may be."

Q "**Fun parties usually get broken up** by a bored security force."

Q "You don't have to participate in the party scene, but it is hard to ignore. **There are all kinds of parties**, though. There are beer-soaked keg affairs, semi-formal invite soirees, and the more colorful affair: cross-dress debutante balls, mustache parties, short shorts parties, and sweaty, '80s post-punk disco dance happenings."

Q "The nightlife at Kenyon, if you like frat parties, is passable, or so I've heard. **If you enjoy hanging out with friends, it's nirvana**. There is enough to do if you don't need fast-paced big city life. The Grille is sufficient, except for its distinct resemblance to a nasty basement. I personally am for the abolition of fraternities on campus, so I can't really comment on frat parties."

Q "**There's enough to do if you're ready to go and find it**. There are always coffeehouses with musicians on the weekends, along with movies that some people like to go to. And of course, there are your frat parties, which are more like dances in the lounges, and then there are the nights where you just hang out with your friends in your dorm."

The College Prowler Take On...
Nightlife

The major party nights at Kenyon are Wednesday, Friday, and Saturday, but if a person really wants to go out, there is usually some small gathering to attend. Fraternities usually invite their friends and correspondent girls over for informal drinking during the week, and most students who opt out of the big parties will either stay in or hang out in one of the upperclass apartments. These are again usually confined to groups of friends hanging out, but the larger size and relative lack of security in these areas makes them conducive to casual partying. One of the few things that Kenyon might have in common with OSU is our love for drinking games. Because Kenyon lacks a bar scene or student union, we use these games as a way to bond. Many close friendships have been given their start over a Beirut table. Security's recent crackdown on these games served more as a validation than a deterrent. All we have to do is play a little more quietly.

For those who actually are of age, the only place where you can utilize 21-year-old privilege is at "the Cove." You won't find the Cove listed anywhere on Kenyon's campus. It was bought by Kenyon and re-opened as the Gambier Grill, although some students refer to it as that. Standard issue Grill by day, at night it turns into the only bar on campus, and the epicenter of 21-and-above nightlife. Let me state for the record that it earns this mantle not because it's the students' choice—it's their lack of options. The bar itself is a window-less room with dark concrete walls, decorated only by random street signs and beer placards. It doesn't bug most students. "It's just where we go," one might say.

The College Prowler® Grade on

Nightlife: D+

A high grade in Nightlife indicates that there are many bars and clubs in the area that are easily accessible and affordable. Other determining factors include the number of options for the under-21 crowd and the prevalence of house parties.

Greek Life

The Lowdown On...
Greek Life

Number of Fraternities:
7

Undergrad Men in Fraternities:
27%

Number of Sororities:
4

Undergrad Women in Sororities:
9%

Fraternities on Campus:

Alpha Delta Phi
Beta Theta Pi
Delta Kappa Epsilon
Delta Phi
Delta Tau Delta
Phi Kappa Sigma
Psi Upsilon

Sororities on Campus:

Epsilon Delta Mu
NIA
Theta Delta Phi
Zeta Alpha Pi

Other Greek Organizations:

Archon Society
Greek Council
Peeps O'Kenyon

Students Speak Out On...
Greek Life

{ **"I think there's more of an emphasis on Greek life than there really is. It really can play as much of a role in your time at Kenyon as you want it to."**

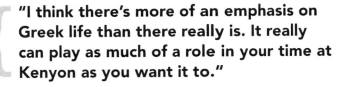 "**Greek life is not what it is on bigger campuses**. Most of the big parties are thrown by frats, and that seems to be their primary contribution to campus life, apart from the occasional blood drive or fundraiser. The only real tension between Greeks and independents comes when housing rears its ugly head. Fraternities do get a sort of housing advantage in campus residences, but it wouldn't be a problem if good housing weren't already in such short supply."

Q "They exist to throw parties, take up tables in the dining hall, make dirty jokes, and gawk at girls. The Greeks also screw up the housing lottery, make freshmen pledges puke, and sing songs about their fraternity. Come to think of it, **I'm sure glad we have them on campus**."

Q "It's definitely there, but not overwhelming at all. It's also not Greek life as you would think of when you think of *Animal House*. **There's definitely always alcohol served**, but I've felt that it's not the overwhelming facet of a frat party."

Q "The admissions office downplays the prevalence of Greek life on campus. Most parties on Wednesdays, Fridays, and Saturdays are Greek-sponsored. However, **there are many alternatives**—coffeehouses and concerts. Fewer people take advantage of these, but they are usually really amazing, and I haven't regretted going to any of them."

Q "**Fraternities do not live in houses**, but rather have sections of the dorms at one end of campus—although, their allotted housing is among the most desired."

Q "One's social life is **not defined by their affiliation**, or non-affiliation, with a certain fraternity."

Q "When my class came in, half of the males pledged; however, the average is closer to one third. In recent years, **that number has dropped because of housing restrictions** placed on sophomores in fraternities.'"

Q "**Sororities play less of a role on campus** because there are fewer of them (four as opposed seven fraternities), and they lack the housing and lounges that fraternities have. About 15 percent of the most recent class of females are active in sororities."

Q "Even for fraternity-run parties, while there is an invite list sent out, **most anybody who comes down will be let in**. Fraternities at Kenyon are not exclusive."

The College Prowler Take On...
Greek Life

Admissions would be hard-pressed to admit this fact, but the Kenyon social scene is still largely dominated by the Greek system. Greeks have the most money and biggest lounges and lodges, and as a result, they are able to throw the biggest parties attracting the largest numbers of people. In many other ways, the Kenyon Greek scene is anything but typical. Unlike bigger universities, a Kenyon student can completely decide to stay out of the Greek system while still enjoying access to Greek parties and the company of their Greek friends. Kenyon is such a close-knit school that fraternities and sororities serve more as clubs than exclusive societies. There are only eight fraternities and four sororities on campus. Since there would be no sense confining their parties just to members, most Greek bashes are open to anyone who would like to come. Invitations are put in people's rooms, but that serves mostly as a way to get the word out.

The rush system also works in a very unique way. First semester, fraternities do not throw any rush events. During this time, frats do everything they can do to get unofficially noticed. There are many parties aimed at freshmen, and individual members also scout prospective pledges. By the time January rolls around, most fraternities have a good idea of who will at least be rushing, but there are always some surprises when it comes time to pledge. The advantage of having a Greek-free life first semester is that students build their own friends without the crutch of fraternities or sororities. This way, they always remain connected to the larger college community.

The College Prowler® Grade on
Greek Life: B-

A high grade in Greek Life indicates that sororities and fraternities are not only present, but also active on campus. Other determining factors include the variety of houses available and the respect the Greek community receives from the rest of the campus.

Drug Scene

The Lowdown On...
Drug Scene

Most Prevalent Drugs on Campus:

Adderall
Alcohol
Cocaine
Marijuana
Ritalin

Liquor-Related Referrals:

90

Liquor-Related Arrests:

7

Drug-Related Referrals:

32

Drug-Related Arrests:

0

Drug Counseling Programs:

Responsible Choices

Students Speak Out On...
Drug Scene

{ **"Kenyon's drugs of choice are cheap beer and Camel Lights. There's a fair amount of pot kicking around, some hallucinogens, a spot of E here and there. It's not really a big scene at all."**

Q "I'm not a drug user, but there are plenty of people who smoke marijuana. I'm sure that there are plenty of drugs, but if you don't have any interest in drugs, they might as well be nonexistent. There are **plenty of stupid decisions people make**, but as long as you make the right decisions, you shouldn't have a problem."

Q "**Don't do drugs**."

Q "There is more cocaine than I thought there would be. I never expected it, but **people say it's easier to find cocaine than marijuana**."

Q "The drug scene has a presence if you are looking for it. **Most people aren't blatantly smoking pot at parties**. They go in small groups to someone's room or somewhere outside. Marijuana is definitely the drug of choice here. I've heard some people do harder drugs, but I haven't seen or heard about that yet. It is not obvious at all, if it exists."

Q "It is evident that pot has its place at Kenyon. It is difficult to gauge the percentage of active smokers, however, it is strong enough that it necessitates acknowledgement. However, **it is also very possible to avoid it entirely** without shutting oneself off from campus activities."

Q "For those into harder drugs, the search is a little more difficult. **There is isolated use of cocaine and ecstasy**."

Q "**Drugs are there for those who choose to indulge**, however, they do not impinge on the lives of those who would rather not partake."

The College Prowler Take On...
Drug Scene

Surprisingly, Kenyon's remote location and general affluence have not fostered any major hard drug scene. Drugs do not come looking for you, but if you want them, they are not hard to find. Pot is a popular drug, and it can fairly easily be found on campus, depending on the season and the standards of the buyer. Many students are casual smokers, but becoming a serious stoner would impede on one's drinking life, and no one at Kenyon wants that to happen.

Most of the other drugs done here are of the hipple variety. Mushrooms and acid come around from time to time, but any coke or ecstasy is kept on the down-low. Since these types of drugs are done behind closed doors, there is a very slim chance that you will have issues with an RA or the campus police, unless you draw attention to yourself. Alcohol is a drug and the most widely used drug, but most people think of the hard stuff when it comes to drugs. The most prevalent drug use probably comes around finals time, when Ritalin and Adderall become two of the most sought after items on campus.

B

The College Prowler® Grade on
Drug Scene: B

A high grade in the Drug Scene indicates that drugs are not a noticeable part of campus life; drug use is not visible, and no pressure to use them seems to exist.

Campus Strictness

The Lowdown On...
Campus Strictness

What Are You Most Likely to Get Caught Doing on Campus?

- Candles in the dorms
- Marijuana
- Parking illegally
- Smoking indoors
- Underage drinking

Students Speak Out On...
Campus Strictness

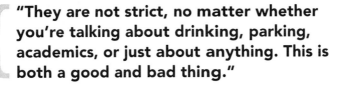

{ **"They are not strict, no matter whether you're talking about drinking, parking, academics, or just about anything. This is both a good and bad thing."**

Q "**Legal policies are very strict**, as well as the academic policies."

Q "**Security has a hard line to walk** and balances it pretty well."

Q "Bringing kegs on campus requires registering them with security. Security is a **presence at the parties where the beer is distributed**. They check to make sure that no one underage is served."

Q "**Security will only bust someone when there is obvious evidence** that they are drinking underage, and the same goes for the dorms. While security makes regular rounds to make sure college policies are being adhered to, they will rarely intercede, unless there is clear cut evidence of a violation."

The College Prowler Take On...
Campus Strictness

There is an interesting yo-yo effect when it comes to campus strictness—some years the security will be lax, others they will be nearly omnipresent. It goes back and forth. The biggest role of security, or at least the most visible one, is monitoring parties. They make sure things are safe, and the festivities end at the right time, but mostly they lurk around and ensure that no freshmen are drinking. In the past, freshmen would put down their beers when they got word of security, and the worst that would happen was being forced to pour out their cup. Now it seems that anyone caught drinking underage gets written up, but no one knows how long this new regime is going to last.

The other complication with Kenyon security is that the Knox County Sheriff exploits the lack of real distinction between Kenyon and Gambier. Students stepping onto streets with open containers of alcohol can easily get written up by the sheriff, and he also hands out the most expensive parking tickets. But it's not like campus security goes out and looks to write people up. They will only take action if they are forced to, so don't draw attention to the fact that you have been drinking if you are underage, and you should be fine.

The College Prowler® Grade on
Campus Strictness: C

A high Campus Strictness grade implies an overall lenient atmosphere; police and RAs are fairly tolerant, and the administration's rules are flexible.

Parking

The Lowdown On...
Parking

Approximate Parking Permit Cost:
$100

Common Parking Tickets:
Parking in faculty parking
Parking in non-spaces

Student Parking Lot?
Yes

Freshmen Allowed to Park?
Yes

Did You Know?

Best Places to Find a Parking Spot

The Norton, Lewis, Watson lots north, and also behind Manning south

Good Luck Getting a Parking Spot Here!

Behind Leonard

Students Speak Out On...
Parking

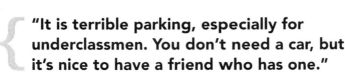

"It is terrible parking, especially for underclassmen. You don't need a car, but it's nice to have a friend who has one."

Q "**There are far too many cars on this campus**, which makes it hard to park."

Q "**South lot is the hardest place to park**."

Q "Parking is not a problem if you don't mind a **five-minute walk to the freshman lot**. I need a car because I couldn't stay in Gambier for the entire year, and I don't like to depend on other people. Don't let other people use you, though, but having a car is definitely a huge benefit."

Q "It's annoying. They make the freshmen park really far away from the freshman dorms when there are perfectly good and open spaces right outside the door. **You don't need a car, but it's really nice to have one** if you want to get off campus and not just take the shuttle to Mt. Vernon. Chances are you'll definitely have more than one friend who has a car."

Q "Upperclassmen are given stickers (either North or South) based on their housing assignment. **About one-fourth to one-third of the students bring cars**, and there is a minor parking crunch because while there are enough spaces to accommodate the drivers, good spaces (closest to the dorms or other popular locations) are hot commodities."

Q "Parking is awful. At the same time, I wouldn't want to see parking lots take over Kenyon's greenery, so I guess we have to deal with it. Surprisingly, parking was easiest my sophomore year when I lived in Mather. We had access to Bexleys and Caples lot and Bexley Hall, and I usually got a spot. **Freshman year, prepare to hike**, junior and senior year, good luck getting a spot at Leonard or Manning—you probably won't. You don't need a car, unless you have an off-campus job, but it is handy. However, enough people have cars (judging from the crowded parking lots), that one is not necessary."

Q "Many similarly small schools do not allow freshmen to bring cars. **Kenyon places no such restrictions on its newcomers**. However, there is a built in deterrent, as freshmen are required to park on the south end of campus, which is at the opposite end from their dorms."

Q "A wrinkle in the parking situation is that because the College and the Village of Gambier are literally intertwined, student drivers are **subject to both the school's parking regulations and those of Gambier**. The spaces on the main roads are governed by the Gambier sheriff."

The College Prowler Take On...
Parking

There are enough parking lots to hold all of the cars at Kenyon, but convenient parking spaces are a little more of a commodity. At a little over a mile long, Kenyon prides itself as a walking campus. The only real use for a car (unless you're very lazy) is for going to and from campus. For these reasons, convenient parking next to dorms and academic buildings is few and far between. For upperclassmen, there is a very small number of very coveted spaces around the historic dorms, but the majority of South dwellers have to park in south lot, which is a down a big hill and pretty far from anything. Those living north fair a little better, with access to both south lot and any of the several smaller north parking lots around the apartments.

Kenyon is unique among small schools in that freshmen are allowed to bring cars and are guaranteed a place to park them. The only problem is that freshmen, who all live north, are given permits only to park in the south lot. This spells a pretty big trek for drivers and can become a big deterrent to getting behind the wheel at all. This year especially, Kenyon has felt a shortage of desirable parking spots. One attempt at compensation was to offer free vehicle registration to drivers willing to park at an even more out-of-the-way new lot, but there were not a lot of eager takers on that one. The College addressed the issue of parking when it drafted its new campus master plan, but students remain skeptical on this point. The plan can be seen at *www.kenyon.edu/masterplan.xml.*

The College Prowler® Grade on

Parking: B-

A high grade in this section indicates that parking is both available and affordable, and that parking enforcement isn't overly severe.

Transportation

The Lowdown On...
Transportation

Ways to Get Around Town:

On Campus

Campus is so small that walking is the only practical way to get around.

Public Transportation

Mt. Vernon Shuttle

Car Rentals

Alamo
local: (412) 472-5060
national: (800) 327-9633
www.alamo.com

Avis
local: (412) 472-5200
national: (800) 831-2847
www.avis.com

Budget
local: (412) 472-5252
national: (800) 527-0700
www.budget.com

Dollar
local: (412) 472-5100
national: (800) 800-4000
www.dollar.com

➔

(Car Rentals, continued)

Enterprise
local: (412) 472-3490
national: (800) 736-8222
www.enterprise.com

Hertz
local: (412) 472-5955
national: (800) 654-3131
www.hertz.com

National
local: (412) 472-5094
national: (800) 227-7368
www.nationalcar.com

Ways to Get Out of Town:

Airlines Serving Columbus

American Airlines
(800) 433-7300
www.americanairlines.com

Continental
(800) 523-3273
www.continental.com

Delta
(800) 221-1212
www.delta-air.com

Northwest
(800) 225-2525
www.nwa.com

Southwest
(800) 435-9792
www.southwest.com

TWA
(800) 221-2000
www.twa.com

United
(800) 241-6522
www.united.com

US Airways
(800) 428-4322
www.usairways.com

Airport

Columbus International Airport approximately 75 minutes from campus.

4600 International Gateway
Columbus, OH 43219

(614) 239-4000

www.columbusairports.com

How to Get to the Airport

Columbus Transportation
(800) 476-3004

A cab ride to the airport costs $100.

Greyhound

111 E. Town St.
Columbus, OH 43215

(614) 221-0577

Travel Agents

AAA Travel Agency
6023 E. Main St.
Columbus, OH

(614) 866-4420

Reynolds Travel
8934 Commerce Loop Dr.
Columbus, OH 43240

(614) 847-8008

Students Speak Out On...
Transportation

"Columbus is 90 minutes away, no fooling. However, with the number of cars floating around, it is easy to get away as there are shuttles to Mt. Vernon. You rarely need to get off campus for material reasons—most often it's psychological."

Q "I thought I'd want to get off campus all the time because I thought Gambier would be constraining, but I was completely wrong. When I do want to get off campus, it is very easy. The **shuttle service goes to Mt. Vernon** pretty much all the time. The shuttle driver is very flexible and will take you almost anywhere. One time I was sick and he took me right back to my dorm. All-campus e-mails make getting to Columbus, the airport, and other cities extremely easy. Chances are, you can catch a ride to pretty much any major Midwestern city when you need to go."

Q "It's very easy to get off campus if you have a car. I need to get off this campus once a week, and remember there is a real world outside of our little town. **If you have a car, that's one less worry** because you can take care of yourself without the aid of another person."

Q "The public transportation within the Gambier Corporation limits consists of the mile-long footpath known as Middle Path, which stretches the length of the campus. Kenyon's campus is small enough that **virtually any spot is reachable with a 15-minute walk**."

Q "**There is a shuttle that runs twice a month to Columbus**—for those who need a taste of the city."

Q "In terms of public transportation out of Gambier, there is a shuttle that drops students off in different points in Mt. Vernon. It runs hourly in the afternoons and evenings on Monday, Wednesday, Friday, and Saturday. **It is no cost to students**, and is a perfect way to escape the hill for a bit, either for a meal, some shopping, or to see a movie."

The College Prowler Take On...
Transportation

As small as it is, you can easily get settled into the Kenyon lifestyle and never feel the urge to leave the hill. Every necessity is right there for you, and it is easy to be lazy about getting in touch with the outside world. With that said, getting out of Kenyon once in a while can be a wonderful thing. Seeing tall buildings and unfamiliar people every so often can help you both relieve stress and appreciate Kenyon even more. While not everyone on campus has a car, almost everyone has a friend who does, so securing wheels usually isn't a problem with a little persistence.

If it's a true emergency, or no one around you is able to lend a car, the College maintains a shuttle service. Four times a week, a bus goes into Mt. Vernon and picks up the students later at specified times, and once a month, the College sends one into Columbus. The only area where transportation really becomes an issue is going to and from the airport. An outside shuttle service provides rides at the beginning and end of major breaks, but the price is almost never worth it. Instead, students take advantage of the "allstu" e-mail function to seek and offer rides. Even in last-minute desperation, these rides will never cost more than the airport shuttle.

The College Prowler® Grade on
Transportation: C+

A high grade for Transportation indicates that campus buses, public buses, cabs, and rental cars are readily-available and affordable. Other determining factors include proximity to an airport and the necessity of transportation.

Weather

The Lowdown On...
Weather

Average Temperature:

Fall:	62.6 °F
Winter:	21.5 °F
Spring:	53.8 °F
Summer:	72.3 °F

Average Precipitation:

Fall:	2.69 in.
Winter:	2.90 in.
Spring:	3.74 in.
Summer:	5.25 in.

Students Speak Out On...
Weather

> "Bring some cool clothes for when you first get here. Remember, it's not cold in August, but bring your warmer clothes, and don't forget your raincoat or your umbrella."

"I made the mistake of bringing about 10 tank tops, only one of which I used, and I used it as fabric for my quilt-making class. Bring sweaters, sweaters, and more sweaters, along with a light, medium, and heavy jacket. I would strongly suggest getting a pair of UGG boots. Don't bring just heavy clothes, though. **The weather can be spastic**, and you'll find yourself taking off your winter coat and putting on a short sleeve shirt and shorts all within the same day."

"Winter lasts from late October to late March or early April, and is characterized by **unrelentingly grey skies, chilly winds, and a great deal of ice**, but not much snow. It is pretty in a masochistically desolate sort of way. Bring a warm coat, a scarf, earmuffs, ankle warmers, and warm boots. However, fall and spring are so beautiful it is quite possible your heart will explode every time you walk outside."

"As for the seasons and your clothing—this is Ohio. **I emphasize layers**—the temperature fluctuates as much as 10 degrees from one hour to the next. Bring tank tops, t-shirts, long sleeve shirts and sweaters. I guarantee you would be comfortable in one of each throughout the course of an average day. Bring mittens, a cute hat, boots, and an umbrella."

Q "Shortly before Thanksgiving break, **the mercury dips to the 40s and 30s** and stays that way until the middle of February."

Q "**It's hot as hell when you get here in August** and the beginning of September, but then it cools off really nicely in September and early October. Winter seems to settle in around mid-October, and then you'll definitely need a warm winter coat, hat, gloves, scarf—the works."

Q "**The first few weeks in late August and early September are hot**, with most days being at least 75, and some touching 90. The beginning of October marks the beginning of fall, and temperatures cool to the 60s on most days. This is also the time when the leaves begin to turn, and the rural campus is at the height of its beauty."

Q "With the exception of last year, which was inordinately snowy across the country, **Kenyon only gets a little snow each winter**."

Q "Dressing for success in this weather pattern requires a heavy jacket for the winter and sweaters in the colder months, but that is bookended by an **almost equal amount of time in shorts**."

The College Prowler Take On...
Weather

Kenyon is in the Midwest, ergo, it has varying weather. This simple distinction often proves a big problem for Southerners and Californians. The weather can be cold, but contrary to the belief of these warm-weather folks, it is always manageable. The first three weeks of school are very warm, and shorts and T-shirts gain exclusive popularity. Things begin to calm down a little bit toward the end of September, and the weather borders on perfect (if a little chilly) through mid-October. It is no coincidence that Parents Weekend falls near Halloween, when it is in the 50s and the leaves turn the campus into the most beautiful place in Ohio. Winter can be long and cold, but in the eyes of this Chicagoan, I know it could be worse. There is snow, and it can be grey outside, but the thermostat rarely drops below the 30s. The trade-off for this dreariness is that spring starts up at full force after the break in March, and the genuine excitement on campus makes this one of the best times of year.

The way to be most comfortable in this climate is to be prepared for both the best weather conditions and the worst. As is listed above, have your shorts and T-shirts available for the earlier portion of the school year, and also after April. Then you need long-sleeved shirts, sweatshirts, and eventually hats, gloves, and heavier jackets. The weather is bearable, but having the proper attire will make you the most comfortable.

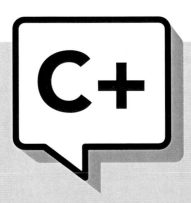

The College Prowler® Grade on

Weather: C+

A high Weather grade designates that temperatures are mild and rarely reach extremes, that the campus tends to be sunny rather than rainy, and that weather is fairly consistent rather than unpredictable.

Report Card Summary

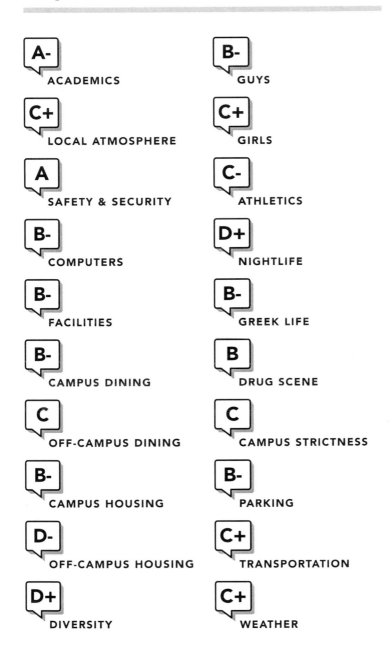

A- ACADEMICS

B- GUYS

C+ LOCAL ATMOSPHERE

C+ GIRLS

A SAFETY & SECURITY

C- ATHLETICS

B- COMPUTERS

D+ NIGHTLIFE

B- FACILITIES

B- GREEK LIFE

B- CAMPUS DINING

B DRUG SCENE

C OFF-CAMPUS DINING

C CAMPUS STRICTNESS

B- CAMPUS HOUSING

B- PARKING

D- OFF-CAMPUS HOUSING

C+ TRANSPORTATION

D+ DIVERSITY

C+ WEATHER

Overall Experience

Students Speak Out On...
Overall Experience

{ **"The people are incredible and have made my college experience wonderful. Kenyon is the perfect college for anyone who is serious about their studies, and life in general. And of course, you'll have an incredible time."**

Q "The best part about the Kenyon experience is the feeling that you get from being there—a feeling that is not quantifiable, and requires a first-hand knowledge of the place to understand. It is not merely one aspect of community, but rather the sum of many things that **contribute to this feeling of comfort and warmth** that Kenyon seems to exude."

Q "Kenyon's a place where all the smart but quirky kids from high school came. We like to learn for learning's sake, but we also like to have fun. We play sports, we sing a cappella, we star-gaze, and we play ultimate Frisbee. There's **definitely something to be said for 1,600 kids who want to spend four years in the middle of nowhere**. We care about our education, but we really care about who we learn with. The people here are awesome, and if you take the time to get to know people, you'll always be presently surprised. Cliché? Maybe, but I think it's true."

Q "The main thing about Kenyon is the **tradeoff between niceness and iconoclasticness**. Kenyon greets you with a warm welcome because everyone here is just so darn nice. But at the same time, since nearly everyone is nice to everyone else, the campus dynamic is just a little more flat than it could be. Speaking for me, the most important thing I was looking for was feeling at home. This is certainly true at Kenyon College, so for me, the tradeoff was definitely worthwhile."

Q "I believe everyone at Kenyon has a 'Kenyon moment' that turns a switch and makes you truly appreciate Kenyon for all its good and bad aspects, because with everything considered, **it is a one-of-a-kind and wonderful place**. As a disoriented freshman, I got lost trying to find the observatory for a Physics lab at 10 o'clock at night during the first week of school. I was somewhere near the athletic facilities, and I asked a lacrosse player if he knew where the observatory was. He said 'no, but I have a car—we can go look for it.' So at 10 p.m., after sports practice, a complete stranger drove me around for a half-hour looking for the observatory. It was a completely unnecessary, yet benevolent gesture that I will always remember. It was one of my first impressions of Kenyon students, and one that they've certainly lived up to since."

Q "If you had told me in the winter of my senior year of high school that I would be spending my college years in Gambier, Ohio, I would have questioned your sanity. In truth, the **three years have met the cliché as the best of my life**."

Q "Kenyon has poisoned me forever. I desperately want to get on with my life, and I never, ever want to leave. **This place is perfect and deeply dysfunctional**. It is not in any way, shape, or form like real life, and why should it be? It's college."

The College Prowler Take On...
Overall Experience

Kenyon College is a small school in rural Ohio. There is no student union, and our "town" is one block long, the weather is unpredictable at best, and half the dorms are said to be haunted. English, our most popular department, sends out its majors to work at supermarkets. However, you still wouldn't be able to ask any current student or alum, "Do you like Kenyon," without setting aside at least 45 minutes for the answer. Kenyon casts a spell on everyone that passes through it—all the things that might initially make it sound unappealing are, in the end, what make the place so special. No one else will ever have a college experience quite like a Kenyon student. Everyone at Kenyon is there for the simple reason that they want to be. They have not come for the glamour of a big city, and they have not come because of an Ivy League name to drop at parties. They have chosen Kenyon in spite of all its deficiencies, or perhaps, because of them. Our isolation simply means that there is nothing to distract us from learning and from each other.

Stuck up on this hill, we really have no choice but to reach out to one another. The reason no one locks their doors is the same reason that most "private" parties are open to the whole campus. As a freshman, you might make a new best friend because you're both wearing the same Yankee's cap. As a senior, you might make a new best friend because you've sat next to each other in the library for three weeks in a row. This unnaturally close community encourages and expects you to open up to all these non-strangers around you.

The Inside Scoop

The Lowdown On...
The Inside Scoop

Kenyon Slang:

Know the slang, know the school. The following is a list of things you really need to know before coming to Kenyon. The more of these words you know, the better off you'll be.

Allstu – An e-mail sent to the entire student body.

The Atrium – The lobby of the library.

AVI – AVI Foodsystems, the campus' food provider.

BFEC – The Brown Family Environmental Center.

The Bank-Box – A black-box theater located next to the post office.

Beta Rock – A south-quad boulder held sacred by the fraternity of Beta Theta Pi.

The Bullseyes – Two rooms with big round windows at the top of Old Kenyon that function as party spots for frats.

The Deuce – Large triple in Hanna used by the D-Phi's for Wednesday night parties.

Division – Wings of the historic dorms allotted to fraternity members.

DormCest/HallCest – Hooking up with someone else in your dorm or on your hall.

Gates of Hell – The two stone pillars that mark the entrance to south campus.

The Grill – The Gambier Grill, the local bar and take-out restaurant.

The Hill – The general Kenyon area, which is set up on a hill.

The Horn – The Horn gallery, a performance space.

Hot Rods – An all-night sandwich chain run out of gas-stations.

Hunan – Hunan Garden, a Chinese restaurant in Mt. Vernon.

Middle Path – The path that runs the length of campus.

Milk Cartons – Off-campus houses that look like milk cartons.

New-aps – The new apartments.

Philo – Philomathesian hall, on the second floor of ascension.

Phling – Philanders Phling, a campus-wide formal held every February in Pierce.

Pink House – A pink house where the Phi-Kaps hold their parties.

Pizza Huts – Off-campus houses that look like pizza huts.

The Pub – Philanders Pub, which serves pizza and is located in the basement of Pierce.

Sexile – Temporarily kicking out your roommate to hook up with someone.

Shock Your Mama – An annual near-naked party thrown by the swimmers.

The Verne – Mt. Vernon, our neighboring town.

Things I Wish I Knew Before Coming to Kenyon

- No matter how big your high school, 1,600 people is simply not a lot of people.
- That a slightly skuzzy Chinese restaurant could become the be-all and end-all of weekend dining.
- Writing is a necessary component of every conceivable academic subject.
- Getting a bat out of a dorm room is more difficult than one would guess.
- It is more difficult to find an open computer during finals than it is to pass the actual tests.
- There truly are a lot of cornfields around here.
- Ramen noodles can be eaten for breakfast, lunch, and dinner.
- A good night's sleep is only for weekends and breaks.
- Making out in public is not cool, even if you are drunk.
- At a school this small, there is no such thing as a secret.

Tips to Succeed at Kenyon

- Sucking up to profs will greatly help your chances of getting into a particular class.
- Starting things off right does wonders for your GPA.
- Don't pre-judge people in frats and sororities; most of them here are very nice.
- Watch yourself—it is easy to get a reputation at a school this small.
- Don't talk too loudly about people in the library—they or their best friend are probably sitting right behind you.
- Make good friends, but keep your independence.
- Rushing a fraternity or sorority does not make you obligated to join it.
- Getting off campus once in a while is good for your sanity.
- Show up to classes, your professor will notice when you are not there.
- Don't let your drinking interfere with your life.

Kenyon Urban Legends

- The basement of Sam Mather Hall contains the actual gate to hell.
- When the church caught fire the flames burned downward.
- Paul Newman (class of '51) donated the $60 million for the new athletics facility.
- *Playboy* once voted us the most promiscuous school in the country.

School Spirit

Kenyon students are insanely proud of their college, but they rarely have occasion to express this. There is a great understood sense of accomplishment in going to Kenyon. We take pride in our high academic environment, and in the underlying trust and closeness of the Kenyon campus. Just because a person is not wearing white and purple does not mean they don't feel this. There is a quasi-rivalry with some of the shinier, but less academic schools in the area (Denison, Ohio Weslyan), but this is usually expressed only through snide comments and the occasional field hockey match. Probably the best indicator of school spirit is our annual Summer Sendoff, but the administration would never put it in our admissions booklet. Summer Sendoff is a day-long party that the school throws the day before the start of finals in May. This is the day when the entire campus comes together in the south quad to drink, barbeque, play games, and generally celebrate being at Kenyon.

Traditions

Frat Tables in Pierce

Pierce's great hall, the school's main dining room, can often serve as a microcosm of Kenyon social interaction. The tables are long enough for people to sit with their extended groups of friends, and fraternities have their own unofficially designated table. The Dekes sit near the entrance, Delts near the conveyer belt, and Betas sit on the heater. There is no real threat for crossing these undeclared boundaries, but a sign of true assimilation to Kenyon is learning which tables in Pierce belong to whom.

Freshman Sing

Freshman Sing functions as the unveiling of the freshmen class to the rest of the school. On their third day of freshman orientation, the entire freshman class lines up on the steps of Rosse Hall and belts out four Kenyon anthems to everyone standing below. Once they have completed these first four songs and earned the respect of the rest of the school, we all join them for a final anthem, and they officially enter the Kenyon community. Freshman Sing can also be used as a preliminary way to scout out the hot frosh.

Friday Afternoon Drinking Club

The Friday Afternoon Drinking Club, or FADC, is not at all school sponsored, but it still draws a fairly large crowd. Held in various locations around campus every Friday at 5 p.m., it has become a mainstay for campus drunks. If you want to want to kick off the weekend early, or at least come drunk to dinner, two dollars will get you all that you need at FADC.

The Gates of Hell

The cornerstone of all Kenyon superstition are the two stone pillars, with a post in the middle, that mark the entrance to South campus. They were nicknamed both because they lead to all of the school's academic buildings, and because they are rumored to be the actual gates to hell. The traditions around them are endless. Some people refuse to walk through the gates at all. Some people never touch the post, some people always touch the post, and some people urinate on the post. There are those that obey the laws of traffic, always going through the right hand "lane," and other that laugh at all these silly gates of hell traditions.

Ghost Stories With Professor Shutt

Humanities professor and campus legend Tim Shutt gathers students around a bonfire every Halloween for a terrifying trek through Kenyon's supposed haunted history. Going year-by-year and dorm-by-dorm, Shutt goes through every death and murder that has ever happened in Kenyon's history, and then tells how the victim presently haunts the school. Even those with the strongest of constitutions have been known to sleep with the lights on after this event.

Philanders Phling

Kenyon is a school with a lot of formal traditions, and a generally informal attitude toward dress and decorum. The formal and informal meet at Philanders Phling, which is an annual winter formal thrown by the school. The ball is held every February, and is one of the most anticipated events of the year. It is also the only time that students really need to worry about looking like lords and ladies, but not about acting like them.

Summer Sendoff

The school throws Summer Sendoff in early May as a sort of last hurrah before finals begin. The day starts with games and barbeques in the south quad, and ends with a concert by a fairly big name band. Students begin their drinking very early in the day, and often don't stop. This is the one day where a person can drink before lunch without getting dirty looks. Whether or not you partake in the debauchery, this is the only day where the entire campus appears truly united.

Vendors on Middle Path

When the weather is nice, and sometimes when it's not, area merchants will set up stands on Middle Path and nearby Farr Hall for student shoppers. Middle Path usually features Amish goods, such as scarves and baskets, as well as fresh local produce. Farr Hall, which is next to the bookstore, usually features slightly more commercial vendors, usually with a hippie twist. There is one man who frequently comes by to sell jewelry and incense, and occasionally used records.

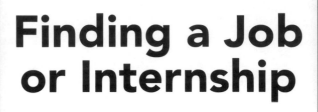

Finding a Job or Internship

The Lowdown On...
Finding a Job or Internship

A liberal arts education, like the one you receive at Kenyon, teaches you how to think; the challenge afterward is getting a job to think for. The CDC is available to help in this endeavor.

Advice

Extern! Kenyon's externship program allows students to shadow someone in a field of interest for 3–5 days over a break. It is a great way to learn about a profession in which you might be interested in and to network. Also, talk to the CDC early and often in your senior year; they are very helpful for seniors.

Career Center Resources & Services

Career counseling, graduate school counseling, resume and cover letter workshops, and e-Recruiting system

Grads who Enter Job Market Within

6 Months: 95%

1 Year: 98%

2 Years: 99%

Firms That Most Frequently Hire Graduates

3M, AG Edwards, ABC, Adobe Systems, Aetna, Allstate, American Airlines, AOL Brand Marketing & Promotions, AT&T, Bank of America, Barnes & Noble, *Boston Globe*, Bureau of National Affairs, CBS, Chicago Public School, Children's Hospital, Citibank, Citicorp, City of NY, CNN, Coca-Cola, Columbus Academy, Corning, Dayton Power & Light Co., Delta, Deutsche Bank, Dow Chemical, DuPont, Eastman Kodak, Episcopal Diocese & Churches, Estee Lauder, Exxon Mobil, FedEx, Fidelity Investments, Fifth Third Bank, Fleet Bank, *Forbes Magazine*, Ford Motor Co., FOX, Gap, GE, H&R Block, Habitat for Humanity, HBO, Houghton Mifflin, IBM, Intel, IRS, JP Morgan Chase, Johnson & Johnson, Lexis Nexis, Mayo Clinic, Merck & Co., Merrill Lynch, Microsoft, Morgan Stanley, MTV, NASA, NBC, *NY Times*, *Newsweek*, NPR, Oxford U. Press, PBS, Peace Corps, Penton Publishing, *Philadelphia Inquirer*, *Pittsburgh Post-Gazette*, Planned Parenthood, Procter & Gamble, Progressive Insurance, Prudential Securities, Qwest Communications, *Reader's Digest*, Riverside Methodist Hospital, Scholastic Inc., Siemens, Simon & Schuster, Social Security Administration, St. Lukes Roosevelt Hospital, *St. Petersburg Times*, St. Vincent's Medical Center, Sun Microsystems, T. Rowe Price, TEK Systems, Texaco, Texas Instruments, Time Warner, U.S. Air Force, U.S. Army, U.S. Coast Guard, U.S. Department of Commerce, U.S. Department of Defense, U.S. Marine Corps, U.S. Navy, U.S. Public Health Service, United Way, Veterans Admininistration Medical Center, Wachovia Securities, *Washington Post*, Wells Fargo, Westinghouse, *Wired Magazine*, World Bank, Xerox, YMCA

Alumni

The Lowdown On...
Alumni

Web Site:

www.kenyon.edu/alumni.xml

Services Available:

Keep e-mail address at Kenyon for 13 months after graduation

Alumni Publications:

Kenyon magazine

Major Alumni Events:

We technically have Homecoming, although it is not very popular. There is a reunion weekend for the intervals of five years the weekend after graduation. This is highly attended.

Did You Know?

Famous Kenyon Alumni

Nick Bakay (Class of '81) – Actor, comedy writer, television producer

Doug Ballard (Class of '76) – Actor

Jim Bellows (Class of '44) – Journalist, editor

Jim Borgman (Class of '76) – Cartoonist (*Zits*), *Cincinnati Enquirer* political cartoonist, Pulitzer Prize winner

Francis Key Brooke (Class of 1874) – First bishop of Oklahoma (Episcopal)

Ken Burgomaster (Class of '91) – Composer

Caleb Carr (Class of '77) – Writer (*Alienist, Angel of Darkness*)

Jay Cocks (Class of '64) – Film critic, Academy Award-nominated screenwriter

James Cox (Class of '60) – Physician, researcher, educator, M. D. Anderson Cancer Center

Meg Cranston (Class of '82) – Artist

Adam Davidson (Class of '86) – Director, Academy Award-winning filmmaker

Edwin Hamilton Davis (Class of 1833) – Archaeologist (*Ancient Monuments of the Mississippi Valley*), medical educator, physician

Carl Djerassi (Class of '43) – Writer, developer of the birth control pill

EL Doctorow (Class of '52) – Writer (*Ragtime, Loon Lake*), Pulitzer Prize winner

Rolla Dyer (Class of '07) – Developer of typhus vaccine, National Institutes of Health director

Eric Gaskins (Class of '80) – Fashion designer

William Gass (Class of '47) – Writer (*Omensetter's Luck, Tunnel*), National Book Award winner

Graham Gund (Class of '63) – Architect

Rutherford B. Hayes (Class of 1842) – U.S. president

Laura Hillenbrand (Class of '89) – Writer (*Seabiscuit*)

➜

Murray Horwitz (Class of '70) – Director and chief operating officer, American Film Institute Silver Theatre and Cultural Center; commentator, National Public Radio

Allison Janney (Class of '82) – Emmy-winning (*West Wing*) and Tony-nominated (*A View from the Bridge*) actor (her voice is also featured in *Finding Nemo*)

Robert Lowell (Class of '40) Poet, Pulitzer Prize winner

William Lowry (Class of '56) – Vice president, John D. and Catherine T. MacArthur Foundation

Robie Macauley (Class of '41) – Writer, editor (*Kenyon Review*, *Playboy*)

Allison Mackie (Class of '82) – Actor

Wendy MacLeod (Class of '81) – Playwright (*House of Yes*), screenwriter

Don McNeill (Class of '40) – U.S. Open tennis champion (singles, 1940)

Paul Newman (Class of '49) – Academy Award-winning actor, philanthropist

Kevin O'Donnell (Class of '47) – Former U.S. Peace Corps director

Oronhyatekha (Peter Martin) (Class of 1863) – Mohawk Indian leader, physician, supreme chief ranger of Independent Order of Foresters

Kris Osborn (Class of '99) – CNN anchor, reporter

Olof Palme (Class of '48) – Prime minister of Sweden

Kristina Peterson (Class of '73) – Former Simon & Schuster publishing executive

William Rehnquist (Class of '46) – U.S. Supreme Court chief justice

Alphonse Rockwell (Class of 1863) – Physician, electrotherapeutics pioneer

Mark Rosenthal (Class of '73) – President and chief operating officer of MTV Networks

Byers Shaw (Class of 1972) – Physician, educator, liver-transplant pioneer

Ned Smyth (Class of '70) – Sculptor

John Snow (Class of '61) – U.S. secretary of the treasury

Edwin M. Stanton (Class of 1834) – U.S. Attorney General and Secretary of War (Lincoln administration)

James Storer (Class of '49) – Retired broadcasting executive

William Swing (Class of '58) – Bishop of California (Episcopal)

Geri Coleman Tucker (Class of '74) – Technology editor, *USA Today*

Bill Veeck (Class of '36) – Baseball innovator, major-league team owner

Fred Waitzkin (Class of '65) – Writer (*Searching for Bobby Fischer, Last Marlin*)

Bill Watterson (Class of '80) – Cartoonist (*Calvin and Hobbes*), Lambda Book Award winner

Matthew Winkler (Class of '77) – Editor in chief, *Bloomberg News*

Jonathan Winters (Class of '50) – Actor, artist, comedian

Peter Woytuk (Class of '80) – Sculptor

James Wright (Class of '52) – Poet, Pulitzer Prize winner

John Celivergos Zachos (Class of 1840) – Pioneering educator, inventor (stenotype)

Nancy Sydor Zafris (Class of '76) – Writer

Student Organizations

Campus Government

ADEPT

Campus Senate

First-Year Council

Greek Council

Judicial Board

Media Hearing Board

Student Council

Student Council Committees and Representatives

Upperclass Committees

Media

56% (Women's interest magazine)

Ascension Films

Kenyon Collegian

Kenyon Daily Jolt

Focus

HIKA

Horn Gallery Literary Magazine

(Media, continued)

KFS (Kenyon Film Society)

Kenyon Visuals

Kenyonion

Persimmons

Reveille

The *Kenyon Observer* (TKO)

The *Voice*

WKCO

Music Groups

Chasers

Cornerstones

Kenyon College Gospel Choir

Horn Records

Kokosingers

Owl Creek Singers

Pealers

Sound Technicians

Stairwells

Take Five

Political

Bioethics Club

Feminist Union of Greater Gambier (FUGG)

Kenyon College Republicans

Kenyon Democrats

Middle East Discussion Forum

Roosevelt Institution

Students for Saving Social Security (S4)

Religious

Agnostic Club

Canterbury at Harcourt Parish

Friday Night Fellowship

Hillel

Koinonia Open Programming Board

Newman Community

Sangha

Zen Meditation Group

Service

APSO (Appalachian People's Service Organization)

Archon Society

Circle K

College Township Fire Department – Student Auxiliary

Kenyon Information and Support Service (KISS)

FLES (Foreign Language in Elementary Schools)

Friends of Hospice

Habitat for Humanity

Hotmeals

Kenyon Student Athletes (KSA)

Safewalks

United Students Against Sweatshops (Kenyon USAS)

The Best & Worst

The 10 BEST Things About Kenyon

1	The people
2	The campus
3	Easy connection with professors
4	Getting a great education without getting it forced down your throat
5	The isolation of the hill
6	Summer Sendoff
7	A cappella concerts in Rosse Hall
8	Fifty cent hot dogs at the village market
9	Everybody knowing your name
10	New athletic center

The 10 WORST Things About Kenyon

1	Facilities
2	Being surrounded by cornfields
3	Parking
4	Language classes that meet nine times a week
5	The isolation of the hill
6	Paltry attendance at sporting events
7	Drinking as social center
8	The incestuous dating scene
9	All-nighters in Gund Commons
10	Graduating

Visiting

The Lowdown On...
Visiting

Hotel Information:

The Kenyon Inn
Wiggin St.
(740) 427-2202
www.kenyoninn.com
Distance from Campus:
On campus
Price Range: $150–$200

The Gambier House
(bed and breakfast)
107 E Wiggin St.
(740) 427-2668
www.gambierhouse.com
Distance from Campus:
Less than 1 mile
Price Range: $100–$155

→

Accent House
(bed and breakfast)
405 N Main St.
(740) 392-6466
www.theaccenthouse.com
Distance from Campus: 3 miles
Price Range: $90–$130

Comfort Inn
50 Howard St.
(800) 480-8221 or
(740) 392-6886
Distance from Campus: 5 miles
Price Range: $70–$90

Curtis Inn on the Square
12 Public Square
(740) 397-4334
Distance from Campus: 5 miles
Price Range: $45–$65

Holiday Inn Express
11555 Upper Gilchrist Rd.
holiday-inn.com
(800) 465-4329 or
(740) 392-1900
Distance from Campus: 4 miles
Price Range: $90–$140

Mount Vernon House
(bed and breakfast)
304 Martinsburg Rd.
(740) 397-1914
Distance from Campus: 6 miles
Price Range: $90–$100

Mount Vernon Inn
601 W High St. (U.S. 36)
(740) 392-9881
Distance from Campus: 6 miles
Price Range: $70–$77

Russell Cooper House
(bed and breakfast)
115 E Gambier St.
(740) 397-8638
www.russell-cooper.com
Distance from Campus: 5 miles
Price Range: $75–$85

Super 8 Motel
1000 Coshocton Ave.
(800) 800-8000 or
(740) 397-8885
www.super8.com
Distance from Campus: 5 miles
Price Range: $60–$64

Take a Campus Virtual Tour

www1.kenyon.edu/tour

Campus Tours

Morning and afternoon interviews and tours are available Monday through Friday, (mornings only on Saturdays) when the College is in session.

Overnight Visits

You may stay overnight (Sunday through Thursday nights) in a campus residence hall. Overnight visits can be especially helpful to your decision-making process.

Directions to Campus

From the North or Northwest

Take Interstate 75 South to Findlay and exit onto U.S. 23/Ohio 15 South. Take 23 South to Ohio 95 East in Marion. Follow 95 East to Ohio 13 South in Fredericktown. Take 13 South to Mount Vernon. Or take Interstate 71 South and exit onto 13 South at Mansfield. Follow 13 South to Mount Vernon.

From South Main Street in Downtown Mount Vernon

Take Ohio 229 East (East Gambier Street).

From the East or Northeast

Take Interstate 71 South and exit on Ohio 13 South at Mansfield. Follow 13 South to Mount Vernon. From South Main Street in downtown Mount Vernon, take Ohio 229 East (East Gambier Street). Or take Interstate 77 South and exit onto U.S. 62 West. Follow 62 to Millwood and exit on U.S. 36 West. Follow 36 to Ohio 308 and turn left (south) onto 308, which leads directly into Gambier.

From the East or Southeast

Take Interstate 70 West and exit onto Ohio 13 North at Newark. Follow 13 North to Mount Vernon. Or take Interstate 77 North to Interstate 70 West. Follow I-70 West and exit onto 13 North at Newark. Follow 13 to downtown Mount Vernon. From there, turn right (east) from Main Street onto Ohio 229 (Gambier Street) to Gambier.

From the West or Southwest

Take Interstate 71 North from Columbus and exit onto U.S. 36 East. Follow 36 East to Mount Vernon. From South Main Street in downtown Mount Vernon, take Ohio 229 East (East Gambier Street).

Words to Know

Academic Probation – A suspension imposed on a student if he or she fails to keep up with the school's minimum academic requirements. Those unable to improve their grades after receiving this warning can face dismissal.

Beer Pong/Beirut – A drinking game involving cups of beer arranged in a pyramid shape on each side of a table. The goal is to get a ping pong ball into one of the opponent's cups by throwing the ball or hitting it with a paddle. If the ball lands in a cup, the opponent is required to drink the beer.

Bid – An invitation from a fraternity or sorority to 'pledge' (join) that specific house.

Blue-Light Phone – Brightly-colored phone posts with a blue light bulb on top. These phones exist for security purposes and are located at various outside locations around most campuses. In an emergency, a student can pick up one of these phones (free of charge) to connect with campus police or a security escort.

Campus Police – Police who are specifically assigned to a given institution. Campus police are typically not regular city officers; they are employed by the university in a full-time capacity.

Club Sports – A level of sports that falls somewhere between varsity and intramural. If a student is unable to commit to a varsity team but has a lot of passion for athletics, a club sport could be a better, less intense option. Even less demanding, intramural (IM) sports often involve no traveling and considerably less time.

Cocaine – An illegal drug. Also known as "coke" or "blow," cocaine often resembles a white crystalline or powdery substance. It is highly addictive and dangerous.

Common Application – An application with which students can apply to multiple schools.

Course Registration – The period of official class selection for the upcoming quarter or semester. Prior to registration, it is best to prepare several back-up courses in case a particular class becomes full. If a course is full, students can place themselves on the waitlist, although this still does not guarantee entry.

Division Athletics – Athletic classifications range from Division I to Division III. Division IA is the most competitive, while Division III is considered to be the least competitive.

Dorm – A dorm (or dormitory) is an on-campus housing facility. Dorms can provide a range of options from suite-style rooms to more communal options that include shared bathrooms. Most first-year students live in dorms. Some upperclassmen who wish to stay on campus also choose this option.

Early Action – An application option with which a student can apply to a school and receive an early acceptance response without a binding commitment. This system is becoming less and less available.

Early Decision – An application option that students should use only if they are certain they plan to attend the school in question. If a student applies using the early decision option and is admitted, he or she is required and bound to attend that university. Admission rates are usually higher among students who apply through early decision, as the student is clearly indicating that the school is his or her first choice.

Ecstasy – An illegal drug. Also known as "E" or "X," ecstasy looks like a pill and most resembles an aspirin. Considered a party drug, ecstasy is very dangerous and can be deadly.

Ethernet – An extremely fast Internet connection available in most university-owned residence halls. To use an Ethernet connection properly, a student will need a network card and cable for his or her computer.

Fake ID – A counterfeit identification card that contains false information. Most commonly, students get fake IDs with altered birthdates so that they appear to be older than 21 (and therefore of legal drinking age). Even though it is illegal, many college students have fake IDs in hopes of purchasing alcohol or getting into bars.

Frosh – Slang for "freshman" or "freshmen."

Hazing – Initiation rituals administered by some fraternities or sororities as part of the pledging process. Many universities have outlawed hazing due to its degrading, and sometimes dangerous, nature.

Intramurals (IMs) – A popular, and usually free, sport league in which students create teams and compete against one another. These sports vary in competitiveness and can include a range of activities—everything from billiards to water polo. IM sports are a great way to meet people with similar interests.

Keg – Officially called a half-barrel, a keg contains roughly 200 12-ounce servings of beer.

LSD – An illegal drug, also known as acid, this hallucinogenic drug most commonly resembles a tab of paper.

Marijuana – An illegal drug, also known as weed or pot; along with alcohol, marijuana is one of the most commonly-found drugs on campuses across the country.

Major –The focal point of a student's college studies; a specific topic that is studied for a degree. Examples of majors include physics, English, history, computer science, economics, business, and music. Many students decide on a specific major before arriving on campus, while others are simply "undecided" until declaring a major. Those who are extremely interested in two areas can also choose to double major.

Meal Block – The equivalent of one meal. Students on a meal plan usually receive a fixed number of meals per week. Each meal, or "block," can be redeemed at the school's dining facilities in place of cash. Often, a student's weekly allotment of meal blocks will be forfeited if not used.

Minor – An additional focal point in a student's education. Often serving as a complement or addition to a student's main area of focus, a minor has fewer requirements and prerequisites to fulfill than a major. Minors are not required for graduation from most schools; however some students who want to explore many different interests choose to pursue both a major and a minor.

Mushrooms – An illegal drug. Also known as "'shrooms," this drug resembles regular mushrooms but is extremely hallucinogenic.

Off-Campus Housing – Housing from a particular landlord or rental group that is not affiliated with the university. Depending on the college, off-campus housing can range from extremely popular to non-existent. Students who choose to live off campus are typically given more freedom, but they also have to deal with possible subletting scenarios, furniture, bills, and other issues. In addition to these factors, rental prices and distance often affect a student's decision to move off campus.

Office Hours – Time that teachers set aside for students who have questions about coursework. Office hours are a good forum for students to go over any problems and to show interest in the subject material.

Pledging – The early phase of joining a fraternity or sorority, pledging takes place after a student has gone through rush and received a bid. Pledging usually lasts between one and two semesters. Once the pledging period is complete and a particular student has done everything that is required to become a member, that student is considered a brother or sister. If a fraternity or a sorority would decide to "haze" a group of students, this initiation would take place during the pledging period.

Private Institution – A school that does not use tax revenue to subsidize education costs. Private schools typically cost more than public schools and are usually smaller.

Prof – Slang for "professor."

Public Institution – A school that uses tax revenue to subsidize education costs. Public schools are often a good value for in-state residents and tend to be larger than most private colleges.

Quarter System (or Trimester System) – A type of academic calendar system. In this setup, students take classes for three academic periods. The first quarter usually starts in late September or early October and concludes right before Christmas. The second quarter usually starts around early to mid–January and finishes up around March or April. The last academic quarter, or "third quarter," usually starts in late March or early April and finishes up in late May or Mid-June. The fourth quarter is summer. The major difference between the quarter system and semester system is that students take more, less comprehensive courses under the quarter calendar.

RA (Resident Assistant) – A student leader who is assigned to a particular floor in a dormitory in order to help to the other students who live there. An RA's duties include ensuring student safety and providing assistance wherever possible.

Recitation – An extension of a specific course; a review session. Some classes, particularly large lectures, are supplemented with mandatory recitation sessions that provide a relatively personal class setting.

Rolling Admissions – A form of admissions. Most commonly found at public institutions, schools with this type of policy continue to accept students throughout the year until their class sizes are met. For example, some schools begin accepting students as early as December and will continue to do so until April or May.

Room and Board – This figure is typically the combined cost of a university-owned room and a meal plan.

Room Draw/Housing Lottery – A common way to pick on-campus room assignments for the following year. If a student decides to remain in university-owned housing, he or she is assigned a unique number that, along with seniority, is used to determine his or her housing for the next year.

Rush – The period in which students can meet the brothers and sisters of a particular chapter and find out if a given fraternity or sorority is right for them. Rushing a fraternity or a sorority is not a requirement at any school. The goal of rush is to give students who are serious about pledging a feel for what to expect.

Semester System – The most common type of academic calendar system at college campuses. This setup typically includes two semesters in a given school year. The fall semester starts around the end of August or early September and concludes before winter vacation. The spring semester usually starts in mid-January and ends in late April or May.

Student Center/Rec Center/Student Union – A common area on campus that often contains study areas, recreation facilities, and eateries. This building is often a good place to meet up with fellow students; depending on the school, the student center can have a huge role or a non-existent role in campus life.

Student ID – A university-issued photo ID that serves as a student's key to school-related functions. Some schools require students to show these cards in order to get into dorms, libraries, cafeterias, and other facilities. In addition to storing meal plan information, in some cases, a student ID can actually work as a debit card and allow students to purchase things from bookstores or local shops.

Suite – A type of dorm room. Unlike dorms that feature communal bathrooms shared by the entire floor, suites offer bathrooms shared only among the suite. Suite-style dorm rooms can house anywhere from two to ten students.

TA (Teacher's Assistant) – An undergraduate or grad student who helps in some manner with a specific course. In some cases, a TA will teach a class, assist a professor, grade assignments, or conduct office hours.

Undergraduate – A student in the process of studying for his or her bachelor's degree.

ABOUT THE AUTHORS

Writing this book was a benevolent challenge for me. It required a lot of time, which as a senior is something I have little of, and a lot of deep reflection about my school and why I love it. I have affection for Kenyon that is indescribable, and I could not imagine being happier anywhere else. I am very proud of my school and this book. A book on Kenyon essentially writes itself, but if it were not for the energy, creative talent, and wit of Zack Rosen, it would not have been possible. Thanks and much respect to Logan Winston, for his unwavering support and guidance. I give my deepest gratitude to my parents, my sister, and my teachers for getting me through Kenyon, and the history department at Kenyon for teaching me to think here. On a lighter note, I am compelled to give shout-outs to those who have made my Kenyon experience—Upper Norton, LSWG, Pink Thunder, and the RA staff.

Jay Helmer
jayhelmer@collegeprowler.com

As an English major, I often question whether or not I will be able to work as a writer when I graduate college. Now that I have actually gotten myself published, I think that I am one step closer to realizing that dream. I have never before had my writing printed outside of school newspapers and YM magazine, and I am still reeling in disbelief at the fact that my name is going to be on the cover of a book. The most important decision I have made in my life was my decision to attend Kenyon, and I hope that my love for the school shows through.

Happy college hunting,
Zack Rosen
zackrosen@collegeprowler.com

P.S. – Extra thanks to my friends and my family, who I hope know what they mean to me. I owe a special debt of gratitude to Jay Helmer for giving me this incredible opportunity and turning "lanky" into a term of affection.

California Colleges

California dreamin'?
This book is a must have for you!

CALIFORNIA COLLEGES
7¼" X 10", 762 Pages Paperback
$29.95 Retail
1-59658-501-3

Stanford, UC Berkeley, Caltech—California is home
to some of America's greatest institutes of higher
learning. *California Colleges* gives the lowdown on 24
of the best, side by side, in one prodigious volume.

New England Colleges

Looking for peace in the Northeast?
Pick up this regional guide to New England!

NEW ENGLAND COLLEGES
7¼" X 10", 1015 Pages Paperback
$29.95 Retail
1-59658-504-8

New England is the birthplace of many prestigious universities, and with so many to choose from, picking the right school can be a tough decision. With inside information on over 34 competive Northeastern schools, *New England Colleges* provides the same high-quality information prospective students expect from College Prowler in one all-inclusive, easy-to-use reference.

Schools of the South

Headin' down south? This book will help you find your way to the perfect school!

SCHOOLS OF THE SOUTH
7¼" X 10", 773 Pages Paperback
$29.95 Retail
1-59658-503-X

Southern pride is always strong. Whether it's across town or across state, many Southern students are devoted to their home sweet home. *Schools of the South* offers an honest student perspective on 36 universities available south of the Mason-Dixon.

Untangling
the Ivy League

The ultimate book for everything Ivy!

UNTANGLING THE IVY LEAGUE
7¼" X 10", 567 Pages Paperback
$24.95 Retail
1-59658-500-5

Ivy League students, alumni, admissions officers, and other top insiders get together to tell it like it is. *Untangling the Ivy League* covers every aspect—from admissions and athletics to secret societies and urban legends—of the nation's eight oldest, wealthiest, and most competitive colleges and universities.

Need Help Paying For School?

Apply for our scholarship!

College Prowler awards thousands of dollars a year to students who compose the best essays. E-mail scholarship@collegeprowler.com for more information, or call 1-800-290-2682.

Apply now at ***www.collegeprowler.com***

Tell Us What Life Is Really Like at Your School!

Have you ever wanted to let people know what your college is really like? Now's your chance to help millions of high school students choose the right college.

Let your voice be heard.

Check out **www.collegeprowler.com** for more info!

Need More Help?

Do you have more questions about this school? Can't find a certain statistic? College Prowler is here to help. We are the best source of college information out there. We have a network of thousands of students who can get the latest information on any school to you ASAP. E-mail us at info@collegeprowler.com with your college-related questions.

E-Mail Us Your College-Related Questions!

Check out *www.collegeprowler.com* for more details.
1-800-290-2682

Write For Us!
Get published! Voice your opinion.

Writing a College Prowler guidebook is both fun and rewarding; our open-ended format allows your own creativity free reign. Our writers have been featured in national newspapers and have seen their names in bookstores across the country. Now is your chance to break into the publishing industry with one of the country's fastest-growing publishers!

Apply now at **www.collegeprowler.com**

Contact editor@collegeprowler.com or call 1-800-290-2682 for more details.

Pros and Cons

Still can't figure out if this is the right school for you?
You've already read through this in-depth guide; why not
list the pros and cons? It will really help with narrowing down
your decision and determining whether or not
this school is right for you.

Pros	Cons
....	....
....	....
....	....
....	....
....	....
....	....
....	....
....	....
....	....
....	....
....	....
....	....
....	....

Pros and Cons

Still can't figure out if this is the right school for you?
You've already read through this in-depth guide; why not
list the pros and cons? It will really help with narrowing down
your decision and determining whether or not
this school is right for you.

Pros	Cons
....	....
....	....
....	....
....	....
....	....
....	....
....	....
....	....
....	....
....	....
....	....
....	....

Notes

....

....

....

....

....

....

....

....

....

....

....

....

....

Notes

Notes

....

....

....

....

....

....

....

....

....

....

....

....

....

Notes

....

....

....

....

....

....

....

....

....

....

....

....

....

....

Notes

Notes

Notes

....

....

....

....

....

....

....

....

....

....

....

....

....

Notes

Notes

....

....

....

....

....

....

....

....

....

....

....

....

....

....

Notes

Notes

....

....

....

....

....

....

....

....

....

....

....

....

....

Notes

Notes

....

....

....

....

....

....

....

....

....

....

....

....

....

Notes

Notes

....

....

....

....

....

....

....

....

....

....

....

....

....

Notes

Notes

....

....

....

....

....

....

....

....

....

....

....

....

....

Notes

....

....

....

....

....

....

....

....

....

....

....

....

....

....

Notes

....

....

....

....

....

....

....

....

....

....

....

....

....

Notes

....

....

....

....

....

....

....

....

....

....

....

....

....

....

Notes

....

....

....

....

....

....

....

....

....

....

....

....

....

Notes

....

....

....

....

....

....

....

....

....

....

....

....

....

Notes

....

....

....

....

....

....

....

....

....

....

....

....

....

Notes

....

....

....

....

....

....

....

....

....

....

....

....

....

....

Notes

....

....

....

....

....

....

....

....

....

....

....

....

....

Notes

....

....

....

....

....

....

....

....

....

....

....

....

....

Notes

....

....

....

....

....

....

....

....

....

....

....

....

....

Notes

....

....

....

....

....

....

....

....

....

....

....

....

....

Albion College
Alfred University
Allegheny College
American University
Amherst College
Arizona State University
Auburn University
Babson College
Ball State University
Bard College
Barnard College
Bates College
Baylor University
Beloit College
Bentley College
Binghamton University
Birmingham Southern College
Boston College
Boston University
Bowdoin College
Brandeis University
Brigham Young University
Brown University
Bryn Mawr College
Bucknell University
Cal Poly
Cal Poly Pomona
Cal State Northridge
Cal State Sacramento
Caltech
Carleton College
Carnegie Mellon University
Case Western Reserve
Centenary College of Louisiana
Centre College
Claremont McKenna College
Clark Atlanta University
Clark University
Clemson University
Colby College
Colgate University
College of Charleston
College of the Holy Cross
College of William & Mary
College of Wooster
Colorado College
Columbia University
Connecticut College
Cornell University
Creighton University
CUNY Hunters College
Dartmouth College
Davidson College
Denison University
DePauw University
Dickinson College
Drexel University
Duke University
Duquesne University
Earlham College
East Carolina University
Elon University
Emerson College
Emory University
FIT
Florida State University
Fordham University

Franklin & Marshall College
Furman University
Geneva College
George Washington University
Georgetown University
Georgia Tech
Gettysburg College
Gonzaga University
Goucher College
Grinnell College
Grove City College
Guilford College
Gustavus Adolphus College
Hamilton College
Hampshire College
Hampton University
Hanover College
Harvard University
Harvey Mudd College
Haverford College
Hofstra University
Hollins University
Howard University
Idaho State University
Illinois State University
Illinois Wesleyan University
Indiana University
Iowa State University
Ithaca College
IUPUI
James Madison University
Johns Hopkins University
Juniata College
Kansas State
Kent State University
Kenyon College
Lafayette College
LaRoche College
Lawrence University
Lehigh University
Lewis & Clark College
Louisiana State University
Loyola College in Maryland
Loyola Marymount University
Loyola University Chicago
Loyola University New Orleans
Macalester College
Marlboro College
Marquette University
McGill University
Miami University of Ohio
Michigan State University
Middle Tennessee State
Middlebury College
Millsaps College
MIT
Montana State University
Mount Holyoke College
Muhlenberg College
New York University
North Carolina State
Northeastern University
Northern Arizona University
Northern Illinois University
Northwestern University
Oberlin College
Occidental College

Ohio State University
Ohio University
Ohio Wesleyan University
Old Dominion University
Penn State University
Pepperdine University
Pitzer College
Pomona College
Princeton University
Providence College
Purdue University
Reed College
Rensselaer Polytechnic Institute
Rhode Island School of Design
Rhodes College
Rice University
Rochester Institute of Technology
Rollins College
Rutgers University
San Diego State University
Santa Clara University
Sarah Lawrence College
Scripps College
Seattle University
Seton Hall University
Simmons College
Skidmore College
Slippery Rock
Smith College
Southern Methodist University
Southwestern University
Spelman College
St. Joseph's University Philladelphia
St. John's University
St. Louis University
St. Olaf College
Stanford University
Stetson University
Stony Brook University
Susquhanna University
Swarthmore College
Syracuse University
Temple University
Tennessee State University
Texas A & M University
Texas Christian University
Towson University
Trinity College Connecticut
Trinity University Texas
Truman State
Tufts University
Tulane University
UC Berkeley
UC Davis
UC Irvine
UC Riverside
UC San Diego
UC Santa Barbara
UC Santa Cruz
UCLA
Union College
University at Albany
University at Buffalo
University of Alabama
University of Arizona
University of Central Florida
University of Chicago

University of Colorado
University of Connecticut
University of Delaware
University of Denver
University of Florida
University of Georgia
University of Illinois
University of Iowa
University of Kansas
University of Kentucky
University of Maine
University of Maryland
University of Massachusetts
University of Miami
University of Michigan
University of Minnesota
University of Mississippi
University of Missouri
University of Nebraska
University of New Hampshire
University of North Carolina
University of Notre Dame
University of Oklahoma
University of Oregon
University of Pennsylvania
University of Pittsburgh
University of Puget Sound
University of Rhode Island
University of Richmond
University of Rochester
University of San Diego
University of San Francisco
University of South Carolina
University of South Dakota
University of South Florida
University of Southern California
University of Tennessee
University of Texas
University of Utah
University of Vermont
University of Virginia
University of Washington
University of Wisconsin
UNLV
Ursinus College
Valparaiso University
Vanderbilt University
Vassar College
Villanova Unversity
Virginia Tech
Wake Forest University
Warren Wilson College
Washington and Lee University
Washington University in St. Louis
Wellesley College
Wesleyan University
West Point
West Virginia University
Wheaton College IL
Wheaton College MA
Whitman College
Wilkes University
Williams College
Xavier University
Yale University